THE HAMMOCK SERIES

LOVE
ILLUMINATED

A Journey to Awaken and Deepen Your Faith

MARLENA COMPSTON

Love Illuminated: A Devotional Journal to Awaken and Deepen Your Faith, Book 1 of The Hammock Series
Published By InspireNations Media
Tulsa, OK

Names: Compston, Marlena, author.
Title: Love illuminated : a journey to awaken and deepen your faith / Marlena Compston.
Description: [Second edition]. | Tulsa, OK : InspireNations Media, [2024] | Series: Hammock
Identifiers: ISBN: 979-8-9901504-0-9 (paperback) | 979-8-9901504-1-6 (hardcover)
Subjects: LCSH: Faith. | Spiritual direction--Christianity. | Jesus Christ--Devotional literature. | Devotional exercises. | Christian life. | Spiritual life. | Spirituality. | BISAC: BODY, MIND & SPIRIT / Inspiration & Personal Growth.
Classification: LCC: BV4501.3 .C66 2024 bk.1 | DDC: 248.4--dc23 & Personal Growth

Cover and interior design by Victoria Wolf, wolfdesignandmarketing.com
Copy line editing by Claudia Volkman
Proof editing by Jennifer Jas, wordswithjas.com

QUANTITY PURCHASES: Schools, companies, professional groups, clubs, and other organizations may qualify for special terms when ordering quantities of this title. For information, email: marlena@marlenacompston.co.

For information on how to create a book club, outreach group, support for this work, consulting opportunities, coaching, or speaking engagements, please visit: marlenacompston.co

You are the very best gifts God has ever given me.
I love you to infinity and beyond.

Contents

PHOTO CREDIT: MARLENA COMPSTON

INTRODUCTION

I WROTE *Love Illuminated* to extend a beautiful invitation for you to seek and pursue a dwelling place for your heart. I desire to share my quiet moments, peaceful times, and calm places where my heart has chosen to dwell. In this busy world, I have found it necessary to seek out and steal away precious moments of solitude for my spirit not only to unwind, but also to seek out that still, small whisper calling me to fellowship with my Heavenly Father.

Some of my very favorite moments are those spent in my hammock, moments spent sitting at the foot of the Cross with my heart completely surrendered to Him. With a soft pillow for my head and wrapped up in my favorite blanket, I feel the Holy Spirit begin to usher in peace as the hammock gently rocks me ... a most definite oasis for my heart. The hammock has allowed me the freedom to have moments alone, to bask in His joy, and, at times, to stain my pillow with tears.

Many prayers have been prayed in my hammock: prayers for my children; prayers for direction, wisdom, and healing; prayers for salvation and deliverance for family members; cries to a Holy Father from a prodigal daughter; and prayers in times of oppression or sorrow. In these moments, my Father reminds me that though I am weak, He is strong. The Lord God and I have spent many a morning with the birds chirping as the sun rises. We've shared many an evening together under a full blanket of stars. This place—my hammock—has proven many times to be holy ground. Today, I pray you will find that place that brings you the very closest to our Heavenly Father. He's waiting for you.

PHOTO CREDIT: JASON HOGAN

GLIMPSE OF GLORY

"He leads me beside quiet waters, he refreshes my soul."

Psalm 23:2–3

SOME DAYS ARE JUST NOT GLORIOUS. The sun shines brightly, and we get burned. The moon sets itself beautifully in the night sky, only to find us awake and unable to sleep. Life can have moments—even days—of unrest. When we feel anxiety and turmoil, there comes a time when we finally yield and give it all up.

It's amazing to me that, in our human flesh, we struggle to "find the answer" to whatever the "issue" is. We must maneuver through relationships, trying not to step on explosive land mines. We put our heart out there only to have it shoved right back at us. Sometimes, letting out a few misplaced words seems to make us feel better than lifting our hands in praise when we're discouraged or feel let down.

As I opened the Word tonight, Psalm 23 came to mind. I turned the pages, and there it was: just ten small words ready to breathe peace into my soul. The words are very clear: He, my Heavenly Father who loves me, tenderly leads and guides me beside quiet and peaceful waters. He, the Lord who created me, refreshes, strengthens, and holds my soul. There is no need to be troubled.

No need to doubt. Just time to sit back and gather peace. To feel the cool breeze on my warm face and know, without a doubt, that tomorrow is a new day.

Thank You, Father God, for a little glimpse of Your glory.

Write out Psalm 23 in your own words.

PHOTO CREDIT: ELI DEFARIA

BREATHE IN LOVE

*"And this is my prayer: that your love may abound
more and more in knowledge and depth of insight,
so that you may be able to discern what is best and
may be pure and blameless for the day of Christ, filled
with the fruit of righteousness that comes through
Jesus Christ—to the glory and praise of God."*

Philippians 1:9–11

WHAT IF YOU CHOSE TODAY to breathe in love and breathe out anything within you that keeps you from *Kingdom living* here on earth? Things like bitterness, unforgiveness, hurt, worry, depression, fear, or jealousy. Just think—if you made a choice to expel those from your soul, they would melt from you and no longer have any power to zap your strength or steal your joy! It is such an easy path to walk when you choose to love—when you choose *not* to accept the invitation to get on the merry-go-round of emotions that threaten to control every single moment of the day.

May you be encouraged today and know that you have the power within you, through Christ, to breathe in love. May your love abound more and more each day.

What is keeping you from breathing in love? What has frozen your heart so you are not able to feel your love abound? Write it below, pray, and let it go today. You deserve peace!

PHOTO CREDIT: MADS SCHMIDT RASMUSSEN

WHAT A MAN

"But let all who take refuge in you be glad; let
them ever sing for joy. Spread your protection over
them, that those who love your name may rejoice
in you. Surely, Lord, you bless the righteous; you
surround them with your favor as with a shield."

Psalm 5:11–12

WHAT A MAN JESUS has always proven to be!

As a baby, Jesus caught the attention of the whole world. As a young teen, He could be found teaching in the synagogue, already showing wisdom beyond His years. As He walked on this Earth, fulfilling His life's calling, He showed great qualities of what a man should be.

First, He was a **servant**. "The Son of Man did not come to be served, but to serve, and to give his life a ransom for many" (Matthew 20:28).

Ever **loyal** to His followers, He always had their best lives at heart.

He **valued children**, and He showed them they were not only valuable but also greatly loved. He was not afraid or "too manly" to show affection. Mark 10:16 tells us that "He took them up in His arms, laid His hands on them, and blessed them" (NKJV).

He allowed Himself to be placed under authority, and he **followed** that

authority to the very end. "Then Jesus answered and said to them, 'Most assuredly, I say to you, the Son can do nothing of Himself, but what He sees the Father do; for whatever He does, the Son also does in like manner" (John 5:19, NKJV).

He was a **great listener** and **friend**.

He was a **compassionate** man who felt the sorrows of those around Him.

One of my favorite qualities about Jesus is that He was, and still is!, **real**. He didn't put up with what I call the "spirit of religiosity." He called a spade a spade.

He didn't choose to hang with the proud Pharisees because He knew they had no intention of swallowing their pride and opening their hearts. Instead, He chose to **spend time** with those who truly mattered and those who wanted a change in their lives. He could not deny or turn away from a repentant heart. Psalm 51:17 states: "The sacrifice acceptable to God is a broken spirit; a broken and contrite heart, O God, thou wilt not despise" (RSV).

Last, He is and will always be a beautiful picture of the perfect **lover** as He extended His arms and breathed His last breath ... for you and for me on the Cross. What a man! What a Savior!

Describe your relationship with Jesus. Do you feel
close to Him, or does He seem far away? Ask Him
to reveal Himself to you through His Word.

....

....

....

....

What a Man

PHOTO CREDIT: ANNIE SPRATT

THE BEST OF INTENTIONS

"Above all, love each other deeply, because
love covers over a multitude of sins."

1 Peter 4:8

THINK OF HOW MANY TIMES we fail at having the best of intentions. I sure have. Both long ago ... and recently. Words spoken meant to help someone that instead left them feeling "less than." The monetary gift I sent a friend in their time of need that instead caused them to feel like a charity case. My intentions were the best, but my gift was not understood or well received. They simply didn't understand the pure love behind it. Remember, however, that time can heal. Love, the Word says, covers a multitude of sins.

Intentions can be misread. Someone can suspect that we have a hidden agenda, even when we have no ill will. The flesh lies. It misinterprets. It looks for something that simply isn't there.

May we love regardless of how it is received. May we seek just the right moments to usher in a word of encouragement or give a gift. And when we have walked in love and learn that it was not received well, we can pray for that heart to be softened by a touch from the Savior of our souls.

Have you ever tried to help someone and your intention was misunderstood? Did you handle it well, or wish you had handled it better? Remember, life can be a learning experience.

PHOTO CREDIT: ISMAEL PARAMO

TODAY IS YOUR DAY
OF SALVATION

"Now is the time of God's favor, now is the day of salvation."

2 Corinthians 6:2

AMAZING WORDS—so much wisdom and truth! Wrap your head and heart around each one. Meditate on them. Allow the Holy Spirit to teach you. If you have not yet taken that step, *today* can be *your* day of salvation.

"You, my brothers and sisters, were called to be free. But do not use your freedom to indulge the flesh; rather, serve one another humbly in love. For the entire law is fulfilled in keeping this one command: 'Love your neighbor as yourself.' If you bite and devour each other, watch out or you will be destroyed by each other. So I say, walk by the Spirit, and you will not gratify the desires of the flesh. For the flesh desires what is contrary to the Spirit, and the Spirit what is contrary to the flesh. They are in conflict with each other, so that you are not to do whatever you want. But if you are led by the Spirit, you are not under the law. The acts of the flesh are obvious: sexual immorality, impurity and debauchery; idolatry and witchcraft; hatred, discord, jealousy, fits of rage, selfish ambition, dissensions, factions and envy; drunkenness, orgies, and the like. I warn you, as I did before, that those who live like this will not inherit the kingdom of God. But the fruit of the Spirit is love, joy, peace, forbearance, kindness, goodness, faithfulness, gentleness and self-control. Against such things there is no law. Those who belong to Christ Jesus have crucified the flesh with its passions and desires. Since we live by the Spirit, let us keep in step with the Spirit. Let us not become conceited, provoking and envying each other" (Galatians 5:13–26).

Are you saved? Do you have total assurance of your salvation? If not, let's take care of that today. Write your prayer below in your own words, or pray the following: "Father God, I confess I am a sinner and in need of a Savior. Thank You for cleansing me of all my sins as I accept Jesus Christ as my Lord and Savior.

Heal my heart, Lord, and fill me with Your Spirit. Amen."

Add the date below your prayer so you will always remember this special day.

....

....

....

....

....

....

....

....

....

....

PHOTO CREDIT: ISAAC QUESADA

MY HEART IS HIS

*"Take delight yourself in the Lord, and he
will give you the desires of your heart."*

Psalm 37:4

LIFE HAPPENS.

It's so easy to allow so many things to pull us. My heart can be tugged to the left and to the right. Here's something I can always count on, though: My heart is His.

As I meditate on the story of the woman at the well, it's so interesting to know that Jesus met her right where she was. She didn't have to "clean up" for Him. He offered her living water; He offered her Himself. She had a lifetime of sin, and it was washed away by His gentle words. Jesus offered precious mercy to a woman who had known nothing of grace or unconditional love. She walked to the well for water and left with a cleansed soul.

She had looked for her life companion and, in fact, met Him that day at the well. She came to the realization that nothing—and certainly no one—could fill her except Him. Life companion, indeed. He would never leave her. He would always provide for her. He would always understand her. He would be the living water in her dry, parched world.

My heart is His. He has never misled me. His Word is truth: He said it, so I can assuredly bank on it being so. He has a great plan, and this woman loves knowing there is a *plan*. As I learn, more and more, to completely surrender to Him, He continues to take my hand and steal my heart. Distractions will surely come my way, but it's my desire and responsibility to keep myself looking forward and to continue to seek His face. It's when I look behind me, at the distraction, that I'm pulled away from the Force that sustains me. Sometimes, life is about adjusting and readjusting. I may not always choose obedience, but I will continue to fall in love with the One who knows me fully.

My heart is His. That's just the way it is. I never doubt or question this fact. I wake up knowing I belong. I go to sleep knowing I still belong.

If you have experienced rejection, loss, upheaval, or devastation, or if you wonder where you fit in this world, He offers life companionship to you as well. Choose life, the Word says—choose Him.

How did this devotion stir your heart? Write
your own love letter to Jesus below.

My Heart Is His

PHOTO CREDIT: AMIR AREFI

CHOOSE OBEDIENCE

"Have I not commanded you? Be strong and courageous.
Do not be afraid; do not be discouraged, for the Lord
your God will be with you wherever you go."

Joshua 1:9

JOSHUA WAS PREPARING the people of Israel to cross the Jordan River. Little did they know the miracles that were in their near future. As we read the first chapter of Joshua, we notice that their hearts were ready. They were prepared to do whatever was asked of them—it was obedience, willing obedience. They wanted a better life for their nation, for their families, and for themselves. After Moses passed away, God placed Joshua in charge, and Joshua took this responsibility very seriously.

Place yourself in the Israelites' sandals. They weren't any different than we are today. Certainly, the times were different, but they were people who needed homes to protect them from the elements, food for nourishment, and clothing to cover them. They needed God. They needed Him to deliver them safely to their new land.

Lord, help us to choose obedience every time. Not grumble. Not rebel. Not question. I know You will show Yourself faithful, as You always do. Amen.

The question to ask yourself is: Am I living in disobedience or rebellion? Let's repent and choose obedience today.

PHOTO CREDIT: WILL TRUETTNER

TRUST HIS TIMING

*"Trust in the Lord with all your heart and
lean not on your own understanding."*

Proverbs 3:5

THERE COMES A TIME when nothing seems to work out the way you had hoped. You felt the Lord had given you a direction, but now you think you might have heard Him wrong. Could it be that it simply isn't the time He chose for you?

For days now, my heart has been going back to Esther. Esther was in exactly the right place at precisely the right time, but she had to wait to know when it was time to go before the king. She heeded the words of her uncle and waited patiently, and then she was shown great favor when her time finally came to approach the throne. As the story goes, she was instrumental in the deliverance of her people.

What have you been waiting for? Does it feel like your dreams will never be realized? This book is a perfect example of waiting in my own life. I *knew* over a dozen years ago that it would happen—I would write a book! I continually prayed, "God, I love You. I thank You for my life and every blessing."

Today, I am praying, *"God, help me to trust You more, to lean on You more, and to better understand Your ways and Your perfect time. Lord, You know I can get impatient and get in my own way. Place me on that 'cliff of trust' so I must fall backward into Your arms and know that You are going to catch me. You have a plan, a purpose, and the perfect provision for me. I am choosing to trust that plan, purpose, and provision to come to full fruition. Today, I simply place this at Your feet, Lord. That's all I can do. It's possible that all You wanted me to do in the first place was to simply trust You and trust in Your perfect time."*

***Are you waiting for something? Praying for something?
Write it below, and add today's date.***

PHOTO CREDIT: GMB FITNESS

PRESS IN

*"That person is like a tree planted by streams of
water, which yields its fruit in season and whose leaf
does not wither—whatever they do prospers."*

Psalm 1:3

I'M REALLY NOTHING SPECIAL—just an average gal living in
the Midwest. What *does* make me special is the redeeming blood of Jesus—and
my desire to fulfill this call, even though I've run from it. I've asked God to
take it away. I've tried to sabotage it.

The best part about this? God is faithful … even when we're not. His call
is irrevocable. He knows what we're capable of. He knows the talent He has
equipped us with. He knows our boundaries. Our shortcomings. Our worst
fears … and our hearts' desires.

Let's take this even further. I quit going to church for several years. Didn't
want to go. Had been hurt enough. Stepped on. Pushed away. Made to feel
"less than," not valuable. But the real reason is probably this: If I didn't show
up, I could better ignore His call. There. You have it. I was running.

Please read this intently. Allow your heart to "listen" very closely. The
call He lovingly places on our life isn't for us. It's for others. We are to be the
guides. The arrows, if you will, to point others in the right direction. Be salt.
Be light. Be love.

As you can probably tell, as you hold this book in your hands, my days of running are over. I am learning to *fully* embrace this unique gifting of "restoration." Restoring what, you ask? Restoring souls. Inviting someone to receive the gift of salvation. Talking with them about their value and His deep and sincere love for them.

Explaining the cleansing power of the blood of Jesus is powerful. It brings hope. It strips away demonic oppression. It offers eternal security. Life-changing, it is.

God offers deep roots to those who trust Him. He offers living water to those of us who are thirsty. He offers rest, and He takes the heavy burden upon Himself. And ... He offers a home with Him in Heaven for eternity.

Press in. Don't run. Answer His knock. He's been knocking at your heart's door for a long time. Are you ready to answer? Choose Him! He's already chosen you.

PHOTO CREDIT: NGHIA LE

PASSIONATE

"For the Lord is good. His unfailing love continues forever,
and his faithfulness continues to each generation."

Psalm 100:5 (NLT)

IN JOHN 21, we read the story of Jesus asking Peter three times, "Simon, son of Jonah, do you love Me?"

Peter answers, "Yes, Lord, you know that I love you."

Jesus then says, "Then feed my sheep."

It hit me just how *passionate* Jesus was about His calling in life. He was not a man or a Savior to be found passive in any way. He knew who He was and what His game plan was. He didn't waste time on activities that didn't matter. We never see Him cowering in fear, backing away from responsibility, or being out of touch with His beloved disciples and followers.

As I was studying John 20 and 21, I noticed the phrase "and the other disciple, the one whom Jesus loved." Get ready for this little nugget of "amazingness": This is John speaking of *himself*! The Lord had a special way about Him that made others feel deeply loved and valued. It's a bit humorous that John tucked this golden phrase into Scripture for us! You see, Jesus was such a wonderful "people person," such a dear friend and leader, that John was convinced he was loved by Jesus above all!

*My Lord, You are amazing! You are always showing us in Scripture that You were—and still are—in the business of **restoration** and **relationship building**. We can see lovingly scattered throughout Scripture that You are also in the business of **healing lives** and **mending broken hearts**.*

In a spiritual nutshell, Jesus was **passionate** about every single person His life touched. We see His passion, whether He was restoring Peter to complete fellowship with Him or beckoning him onward so Peter could fulfill the call on his life to "feed my sheep." We see another beautiful example of His love when He asked that His mother be taken care of while He was enduring the Cross. And then there is the woman with the issue of blood who "merely" touched the very hem of His garment. He felt the healing power leave Him as she reached out for Him.

He was **passionately focused** on those He loved. He was, without a doubt, **in tune** with those around Him. He wanted to know them. He purposed to make a difference—and a difference He certainly made. He chose the Cross, knowing the pain He would endure. Jesus was a passionate man—a purposeful Savior with a burning desire to reconcile those He loved with His Heavenly Father. The plan worked beautifully and continues to this day.

Father, dial in my heart's focus very clearly and closely to You. Let my purpose and passion be crystal clear. May I wrap my arms and heart around those I encounter and point them toward You and Your purpose for them. Lord God, may my life glorify You. Even through my down times, may my lips sing glory to Your name. May I be assured by knowing that You restore and revive me over and over again. When I turn left, help me to turn right. When I take steps that back me away from You, guide and direct me once again in the direction and purpose You placed on this heart and this life. Amen.

What are you passionately focused on?

PHOTO CREDIT: BEN WHITE

ALWAYS THERE

Heavenly Father,
I know You're always there
Watching and waiting
Knowing I won't wander far
From my Father's eyes
Your love draws me, O God
Back to You time and time again
I lay down my will
And ask only Your will takes place
Dying to self once again
Over and over again
Trusting and believing
Telling doubt and fear to flee
And gently nuzzling my life
Back into the fold of Your love
And exactly where You intend
For this child to be.

What do the words "always there" mean to you?

PHOTO CREDIT: ORLANDO ALLO

LEGACY

*"I press on toward the goal to win the prize for which
God has called me heavenward in Christ Jesus."*

Philippians 3:14

CONSIDER YOUR LEGACY. What are you preparing to leave
your children and grandchildren?

As we get older, we see how precious life really is—and how quickly it goes
by. Ecclesiastes 3:2 speaks of "a time to be born and a time to die." Not only
do I have a desire to leave my family an inheritance, but I also want to leave
them with words they can read long after I have left this world. Prayers I've
prayed over them for years, all my Bibles with every little scribble and date, and
hopefully some wisdom and a bit of knowledge. Not because I am so wise or
even all that knowledgeable but because my Heavenly Father **is**! Every single
written word wrapped up in love just for them.

Look within and begin planning *your* legacy. One day, all that will be left
of our existence will be memories, pictures, words written or spoken to our
loved ones, thoughts about the love and time we shared, and those precious
prayers that will continue for them.

In closing, join me in praying for our children, grandchildren, great-grand-
children, and on and on ... until Jesus returns.

How do you feel about leaving a legacy for your family?
What would you like to be remembered for?

LEGACY

PHOTO CREDIT: ROBERT DANIELS

GEORGE WASHINGTON

*"Jesus Christ is the same yesterday
and today and forever."*

Hebrews 13:8

WAS GEORGE WASHINGTON a Christian? Consider these
words from his personal prayer book, and decide:

Oh, eternal and everlasting God, direct my thoughts, words, and work.
Wash away my sins in the immaculate blood of the lamb and purge my heart by
the Holy Spirit. Daily, frame me more and more in the likeness of thy son, Jesus
Christ, that living in thy fear, and dying in thy favor, I may in thy appointed
time obtain the resurrection of the justified unto eternal life. Bless, O Lord,
the whole race of mankind and let the world be filled with the knowledge of
thy son, Jesus Christ.[1]

I can see him, in my mind's eye, sitting in his presidential office, writing
in his personal prayer book. Someone said of him, "Throughout his life, he
spoke of the value of righteousness, and of seeking and offering thanks for the
'blessings of Heaven.'"

George Washington was born in 1732 and died in 1799 at the age of
sixty-seven. He was born into this world, lived a full and devoted life, and
chose to bow his knee to Almighty God, recognizing his state of being lost
without Him.

The same Heavenly Father who loved and cared for George Washington is the same God who loves and cares for you.

Write a prayer below to your Heavenly Father. Think of someone reading it many years from now. How do you want your love and adoration for your Lord to continue on in words even after you are gone?

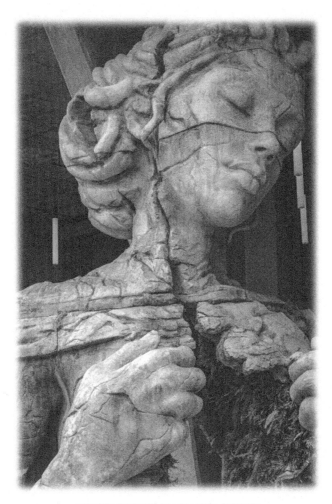

PHOTO CREDIT: MARIANNA SMILEY

BEAUTIFULLY BROKEN

"And she made a vow, saying, 'Lord Almighty, if you will only look on your servant's misery and remember me, and not forget your servant but give her a son, then I will give him to the Lord for all the days of his life, and no razor will ever be used on his head.'"

1 Samuel 1:11

HANNAH HAS BEEN ON MY MIND LATELY. The Word speaks of Hannah weeping before God. Have you ever found yourself on your knees ... hot tears streaming down your face, pouring your heart out to God? Hannah's heart was broken. She prayed for a son and sincerely believed God would provide ... now she was completely broken before Him. You see, Hannah was a wife and unable to present her husband with a child. Hannah, weeping and childless, had one desire, and she laid it out before Him. She knew fully that her Lord was the One who could provide her with the very desire she longed and prayed for.

God did answer Hannah's prayers, and she was blessed with a son, Samuel. After she weaned Samuel, she dedicated him completely to the Lord's service. I find it so humbling to know that she prayed, believed, received the desire of her heart, and then lovingly opened her arms completely to give that same gift of her son right back to her Lord. What an example she gave us!

I must admit that, as a mother, it's difficult to think of giving up time with my children. It's just natural to want to hold on to them—even when they're grown. My oldest son enlisted as a Marine. There came a time when I had to hug him goodbye and send him to a country far away from the comforts and safety of home. I admit ... I didn't want to. I wanted to hold on and keep him close. Through my inner struggle with this, it came to me that **God** loved my children long before I even knew them. And He loved me enough to share them with me. What an honor. What a huge blessing.

Lord, I can't fully understand Hannah's sacrifice, but I certainly thank You for her example. Help me to have a heart like Hannah's. Lord, I want to thank You for unselfishly sending Your own Son to be beautifully broken for us. His sacrifice made it possible for us to have a path and an open door to You.

Are you a parent? Have you ever felt the way I did? Are you praying to become a parent?

I encourage you to use the space below to pour your heart out like Hannah did. God honored her prayer of faith. If He would do this for Hannah, He can do it for you.

....
....
....
....
....
....

PHOTO CREDIT: DICSON

ABOVE THE FRAY

"Even youths grow tired and weary, and young men stumble and fall; but those who hope in the Lord will renew their strength. They will soar on wings like eagles; they will run and not grow weary, they will walk and not be faint."

Isaiah 40:30–31

MY FORMER BOSS WELDON, once said to me, "Always stay above the fray." I researched the phrase *above the fray* because I wanted to clearly understand its meaning. I discovered that *above the fray* means "to not let the chaos or hubbub surrounding you affect you."

If we go to the Word, we can find many examples of people who stayed "above the fray." Jesus was the very best at this and serves as our best example of staying above it all. Only once did he seem to lose his cool—and even then, He didn't sin. This was when he cleared out the moneychangers from the temple. Think about all of Jesus's actions. He cared deeply. He continually sacrificed His time and His energy. He always guided people toward truth. He always sought the will of His Father, never selfishly demanding His own will. He certainly stayed "above the fray," even though the hubbub and drama were always around Him.

One specific scene grabs my heart: when he was in the midst of a crowd of people pushing and pulling him from all sides. One ill and desperate, determined woman was able to touch not only His garment but also His heart. The moment she reached out in her weakness, all the while possessing great faith, the Word says that virtue left Jesus, even with all those people pulling and pressing on him. He was **above the fray**, and he **knew** power had left Him and poured out toward someone who needed His help.

Isn't that *awesome* news? He is *moved with compassion* to meet our needs. He *redeems our messes*, and He *longs* to solve our problems. We can look through Scripture and see promise after promise of what He desires for us. So many of us grew up on a religious diet of "hellfire and brimstone," and now we need to allow the Holy Spirit to refocus us and help us finally understand fully His mercy, His grace, and His forgiveness.

When life gets tough—and it does—when there is "hubbub" all around—and there is—may we **choose to rise above the fray**. The prophet Isaiah speaks of mounting up on wings like eagles—get a full picture of that! Eagles simply S-O-A-R. That's what they *know* to do. They don't try; they just do it naturally.

Lord God, help us to spread our wings of faith as we learn to abide in Your "nest" of salvation, security, and assurance of eternity. Help us live the way You did and love the way You do.

What is holding you back or even holding you down? Do you need to rise above the fray? Today, choose to SOAR and not let the circumstances of life keep you down. Your obedience to Him and your happiness MATTER!

PHOTO CREDIT: GEETANJAL KHANNA

AN OUTSTRETCHED HAND

"Asa's heart was fully committed to the Lord all his life."

2 Chronicles 15:17b

Father, remind me of what it means to have a heart "fully committed."
That's the place where my head stops thinking so much and my heart
yields. It's where the loss of something or someone in my life isn't nearly
as painful if I can just tap into the faith in my heart and carefully ...
slowly ... push through, realizing the incredible future You have waiting
ahead for me.

FOR WEEKS, MY HANDS HELD ON TIGHTLY to what
I wanted, but the Lord clearly said, "LET GO."

"But, Lord, I can't see past tomorrow," I said. "I'm having a difficult time
trusting Your Word, though I know You've always been faithful."

Second Chronicles tells us that Asa's heart was fully committed ... all his
life. In Matthew 6:33, we are encouraged to seek first His kingdom and His
righteousness, and *all* these things will be added to us. What is your definition
of *all*? Peace? Forgiveness? A companion? A family? Health? Every one of us
has an *all* definition.

My favorite Scripture and one that I cling to is Psalm 37:4. "Take delight in the Lord, and he will give you the desires of your heart." This Scripture just seems to complement Matthew 6:33. God has given us **so many promises** that I wonder how we ever find ourselves feeling alone … empty … forgotten … unforgiven? We've all been there.

My mother used to say there's no such thing as a "utopia," but I've always felt that utopia is found within our own heart—fully committed for life to the very One who knows us so completely. It's not about a church or the pew you sit in every week. It's not about a denomination. It's this ongoing, beautiful walk between here and Heaven that holds us close … during the good times and the bad.

Father, I choose to cast all my cares on You, for You care for me. I believe, by faith, in Your perfect work and Your perfect will. Tomorrow is a new day, and Your Word says Your mercies are NEW every morning. Clean slate. Fresh start. Healed heart and an outstretched hand reaching for You instead of holding onto something that You've lovingly whispered to "let go." Make it easier to understand, Lord. Help any loss in my life to make sense to my heart. Allow the sun to shine again and remind me, once more, of the depth of Your love and the total and unfathomable depth of Your understanding of any loss that we might experience in this life. Amen.

Rewrite the above prayer and make it your very own.

....

....

....

PHOTO CREDIT: JOHANN WALTER BANTZ

BOXING SHADOWS

"Whoever dwells in the shelter of the Most High will rest in the shadow of the Almighty. I will say of the Lord, 'He is my refuge and my fortress, my God, in whom I trust.'"

Psalm 91:1–2

LIFE CAN CERTAINLY throw us a punch. Ever find yourself backed into a corner and boxing at dark shadows? One shadow might be named Fear. Fear—that ugly shadow that rears its nasty head and causes you to lose your center. Typically, the closest companion of Fear is his partner What If. He causes you to question and doubt and imagine. Another shadow might be named Abandonment. That irrational shadow has been allowed to linger for much too long, continually taking you back to past wounds, echoing and replaying them like a broken record. And let's not forget Depression—that scroungy dog waiting to pounce upon your heart and nerves at your weakest moments. What about Loss, the underlying voice that says you'll always lose those you love. Over and over ... boxing shadows ... a jab to the left ... a jab to the right.

There *is* good news for us—a shining light at the end of a dark tunnel, a glimmer of hope against a dark corner full of musty shadows. God's Word, once again, brings us supernatural comfort. One of my favorite Scripture passages is Psalm 91:1–2, quoted at the beginning of this devotion.

Reflect with me on that amazing and comforting promise: "Whoever" dwells (or places themselves) in the shelter of the Most High. Do you see it? We will rest in *His* shadow—the shadow of the Almighty, our peace, our deliverer, our refuge, and the One who wants to be our fortress. There will be no boxing shadows of fear, abandonment, or loss in *that* place. His Word says we will rest. There is no fighting or even losing the battle. We simply can rest ... and trust, protected by our loving Father. Our promise is clear. He will never leave us, nor will He ever abandon us. No more boxing empty, powerless shadows; the fight has already been called. The winner has already been named.

Where is your refuge? Where do you go for comfort?

....
....
....
....
....
....
....
....
....
....
....
....
....

PHOTO CREDIT: CHARLOTTE KARLSEN

DIVE IN

"Forget the former things; do not dwell on the past.
See, I am doing a new thing! Now it springs up;
do you not perceive it? I am making a way in the
wilderness and streams in the wasteland."

Isaiah 43:18–19

THE HOLY SPIRIT SPOKE to my heart, and I heard him say, "Why do you continue to wade in a river when you can swim in the ocean?"

What the Lord plans for us is so much bigger, so much wider, and so much deeper than what we could even begin to dream. When you are in a place in life where it seems that everywhere you turn, a door is closed in your face, then maybe it is high time to move forward and test new waters … as He leads. Sometimes, we allow ourselves to remain in a place because we're in a comfort zone and don't want to make a change. Sometimes, we're miserable within this comfort zone, but we wrongly determined that we must remain.

No! The Lord says He is doing a new thing! He is making a way in the wilderness of our lives and preparing the wastelands of our hearts to enjoy a new, fresh infilling of His Spirit. Indeed, forget the former things and do not dwell on them any longer. Dive into the ocean of the fantastic future He has planned for you!

If you ever find yourself fighting for something that is LESS THAN what God wants for you, instead choose His path, where you can live in peace. Write a letter to yourself about these exact things.

....
....
....
....
....
....
....
....
....
....
....
....
....
....
....
....
....
....
....
....
....
....

PHOTO CREDIT: RED ZEPPELIN

THE KINGDOM OF GOD

"But seek first his kingdom and his righteousness,
and all these things will be given to you as well."

Matthew 6:33

"HIS KINGDOM"–HIS HOLY PRESENCE. His desire to
protect us. His provision to provide for us. Jesus simply says, "Seek." The
Kingdom of God is the very glue we need to hold it all together. Within this
Kingdom are many rooms—rooms filled with so many things. Peace, for one.
Nothing and no one can offer us peace like He can. With Him, we have peace.
Without Him, we may never experience peace the way He longs for us to
experience it. We can walk around thinking we have it all together and then
realize we have avoided Him for too long. He is a loving and, yes, jealous God.
He won't share us for long. His gentle, loving, and heavenly hand will reach
out to us and guide us back again and again.

"His righteousness"—only He could have made us righteous. Placed his
stretched arms across a wooden cross and willingly laid the foundation for our
future. He purchased us with every drop of His blood ... knowing the pain,
accepting the temporary separation ... then knowing He had fully paid the
price, He took His last breath. His Father had a divine plan for us. Our value
to Him is immeasurable, and His love for us is never ... ever ... ending.

"All these things"—I don't want material items that will turn to dust in an instant. I want a future that is full of His Spirit. I want to know that the Comforter is right beside me, *know* that I am following His will, right in the middle of it, and certainly not following my own.

"Will be given to you"—that's a promise. Read the Scripture again. Seek first His Kingdom, His righteousness, and *all* these things will be given ... TO YOU.

How can you begin today to seek His Kingdom? What do you need to do to start on the road to a closer walk with Him?

....
....
....
....
....
....
....
....
....
....
....
....
....
....
....
....

PHOTO CREDIT: OLGA NAYDA

PERMISSION GRANTED

"You will show me the way of life, granting me the joy of your presence and the pleasures of living with you forever."

Psalm 16:11 (NLT)

TODAY IS A NEW DAY—a new day to give yourself *permission* to be happy. Bottom line: We all make mistakes. We've all been hurt, wounded, scarred, bruised, abandoned, and left high and dry—and today is the day to stop the madness and realize it is the first day of the rest of our lives. I know too many people who are still hurting from things that happened to them *years* ago. I admit, I've been that person, too, *but no more*!

It's time to draw your line in the sand and boldly say, "I AM GOING TO BE HAPPY!" Quit worrying about what other people think. Quit finding more comfort in sad tears than in tears of joy.

Years back, I attended a divorce recovery class. I remember sitting in a large circle of women of all ages. Many were crying and upset. I started crying, too, because the oppression was so heavy in the room. I thought, *Maybe this is a good thing—maybe it is cleansing and healing, so bring it on!*

Then, several of the women began to talk about their divorces. Some had been divorced for five years, ten years—and one for even thirty-five years! *Oh, my goodness!* God has **healing** for our hearts. We absolutely were not created to carry around burdens that bend our shoulders down below our knees (and it looks kind of weird, too, walking like that!). We just weren't built to function that way.

A friend of mine told me that he tells his clients who are carrying a lot of guilt that he's going to place a backpack on them and weigh it down with heavy rocks. Eventually, he advised them, they would get tired of "carrying the weight" and finally lay that backpack down.

So, guess what? *Today* is the day to take off your backpack full of rocks (guilt) and lay them down. Where in the world did you get the idea that you're supposed to feel guilty and condemned all the time? Things in your past that you have confessed (see 1 John 1:9) are now as far as the east is from the west (see Psalm 103:12). There is *victory*, and we no longer need to be a victim of:

ourselves

others

past mistakes

future challenges

Shake each of them off like a dirty suit! Instead, I encourage you to put on your "glory suit" and know that while you will mess up sometimes, you will never allow guilt or *condemnation* or *fear* or *sorrow* or *anger* or *anything else* to keep you from experiencing the full joy of your salvation.

Have you had a vacation lately? If not, it's high time you sit down and decide what you can do this week to make yourself H-A-P-P-Y! It's time to start living on your "happy cloud." Understand that no one else will make you happy—it's your job, with the help of the Holy Spirit. Discover your "happy cloud" inside your own heart—and LIVE!

PERMISSION GRANTED THIS DAY TO BE GLORIOUSLY HAPPY!

What does your HAPPY CLOUD look like today?

PHOTO CREDIT: ALEX AZABACHE

THE BRIDGE

*"Return to your fortress, you prisoners of hope; even now
I announce that I will restore twice as much to you."*

Zechariah 9:12

THIS DEVOTION IS A REMINDER that our Father in
Heaven is still in the business of building and reconstruction. He is the very
best at making our crooked roads straight again. All He asks for is a willing
heart. During these times of "heart renovation," He allows our hearts to be
hollowed out so He can rebuild them and refill us with the healing power
of His Holy Spirit. He allows issues within us to be exposed so we can be
regenerated and renewed, thus restoring our hope, joy, and fellowship with
Him. Going through this isn't very glorious, but the process is both necessary
and well worth the journey.

Disappointment can push you into the wrong place in life. It can cause
you to make choices you wouldn't normally make, do things you wouldn't
normally do, and be someone God never intended you to be. Disappointment
can distract you and cause you to want to give up, *but then God. ...* He always
has a bridge to reconnect your heart to Him. He's working in the midst of
every disappointment in your life, no matter how large or how small. He's
building a foundation; he's stretching far and wide across your devastation to
bring you right back to Him.

Catch a glimpse of the Father looking down the road at His prodigal child. Keep your eyes and heart straight ahead and cross that bridge He's built for you. You're almost home.

Do you feel that your life needs restoration? Ask God to begin restoring those broken pieces. Make a list of the areas that are broken, and give them to Him to restore and rebuild.

PHOTO CREDIT: DAVID PERRY

MANIPULATION ... NO MORE

"Do not take advantage of each other, but fear your God. I am the Lord your God."

Leviticus 25:17

THIS IS YOUR HEADS-UP regarding manipulation. Do *not* let anyone manipulate you. Your life is yours. Other people may not like your decisions or your actions, but it is *your life*. God takes care of us in His way and on His timeline. Trust Your Heavenly Father to bring you what you need when you need it. Do not let someone else tell you what you must have or what you must walk away from. *See clearly through your own eyes* and take your next steps toward freedom and far away from manipulation.

Look up the definition of **manipulation.** *Become familiar with what it is. Then determine not to allow yourself to be manipulated, nor to manipulate others.*

PHOTO CREDIT: ALEX SHUTE

BANISH FEAR

"So do not fear, for I am with you; do not be dismayed,
for I am your God. I will strengthen you and help you;
I will uphold you with my righteous right hand."

Isaiah 41:10

FEAR CAN BE A POWERFUL FORCE that manipulates our senses until we grab hold of truths that dissipate the fear. FEAR paralyzes. FEAR cripples. FEAR is a thief of precious moments. FEAR is a liar. FEAR is not your friend. God did not give us a spirit of fear!

Imagine placing your fear in a box today. Then, cast this box full of fear far from you. It is not yours—and it never was. When you realize that you are an OVERCOMER, you will learn that fear has NO POWER over you. When you realize that you are a child of the King, fear can no longer hold you. When you begin exposing truth and light, fear falls away.

Write out these words: "For God has not given us a spirit
of fear, but of power and of love and of a sound

*mind" (2 Timothy 1:7, NKJV). I encourage
you to memorize this verse.*

PHOTO CREDIT: JOSH HILD

THE DREAM IS REAL

*"Do you not know? Have you not heard? The
Lord is the everlasting God, the Creator of the
ends of the earth. He will not grow tired or weary,
and his understanding no one can fathom."*

Isaiah 40:28

WHAT IS YOUR DREAM? Write it down. Take it to our Heavenly
Father. Listen. Watch as He lovingly unfolds His plan. He's never early. He's
never late. He's always right on time.

*What are your dreams? Take some time to write
them down. Prioritize them if you need to!*

....

....

....

PHOTO CREDIT: QUINTEN DE GRAAF

THE CREATIVE
MIND OF GOD

*"You keep track of all my sorrows. You have
collected all my tears in your bottle. You
have recorded each one in your book."*

Psalm 56:8 (NLT)

HAVE YOU EVER THOUGHT, *I don't believe God is interested in
the little things in my life?*

Let me expound on just how interested He truly is. Let's consider the fact
that fifty thousand cells in your body will die and be replaced with new cells,
all while you're reading this sentence! It's His plan for the regeneration of our
cells and blood! Did you know He designed your left lung smaller than your
right lung to make room for your heart? What a loving Father to hollow out
a very special place for our heart!

He knew our eyes needed protection from dust, so He designed our eyelids
to blink in a way that protects our eyes. The average person blinks approxi-
mately twenty-three thousand times a day, or 6.25 million times in a year. And
did you know that only eight weeks after a baby is conceived, the bones begin to
replace cartilage? At twelve weeks, their little organs are in place. At eighteen
weeks, they begin to hear, and at twenty-three weeks, their little fingerprints

begin to form. What a miraculous, artistic way of showing His love from the very beginning!

As you can see, God is *very* interested in the little things. He's also interested in the condition of your heart and soul. He's concerned about the state of your mind. He's concerned about and wants to be a part of all the decisions in your life. Invite Him into your life every single day. Talk to Him about the details of your life. Praise Him today for His grand design of Y-O-U! Remember that before you were a twinkle (or a blink) in your parents' eyes, He already had a beautiful, original design with your name carved upon it.

Father, thank You for Your creative mind that has been thinking of us all along. Help us to know You more—deep within our hearts—to see Your face and to understand You more clearly. Lord, we want to know You more. Amen.

Don't you love knowing that God is interested in the details of your life? He even stores your tears in Heaven; He doesn't dismiss them. He is our caring, intimate God of details.

PHOTO CREDIT: MATHILDA KHOO

HIS MASTERPIECE

"He has made everything beautiful in its time. He has also set eternity in every human heart; yet no one can fathom what God has done from beginning to end."

Ecclesiastes 3:11

IT IS AMAZING TO ME how many people are so hard on themselves. They criticize every little part of themselves. But God knit each of us together in our mother's womb, according to Psalm 139. Realize today that no one in the world has the exact same sparkle in their eyes as you do. Look at your fingertips and realize that the God of all creation loved you so much that He made a one-of-a-kind pattern for your fingerprints, never to be duplicated again. Look at that beautiful smile on your face, and know that no one smiles just like you do! The tone of your voice, the touch of your hand, the way you walk, and the gifts placed within you—they are all uniquely you.

You are His masterpiece! He not only made you special, but He also made a special way for you to be in fellowship with Him. If you've never experienced that wonderful washing of your spirit, that washing away that takes place when you hand over all your heartache and disappointments ... all those things that make you feel less than enough—let today be *that* day. 1 John 1:9 says, "If we confess our sins, He is faithful and just to forgive us our sins and to cleanse us from all unrighteousness" (NKJV). It is so simple. Give Him the very things

He's already paid for; you no longer have to carry them. You were never meant to carry them! Let today be the day that you accept yourself just the way you are and accept Him fully for who HE is.

Come on! Let those gorgeous eyes twinkle ... that extraordinary smile beam across your face ... and just bask in the beautiful truth that not only are you so very lovable but also He loves you so very much! Your heart can rest always in the palm of His hand. He is faithful and trustworthy. He is the glorious Artist and Creator who will never fail you. You are His precious masterpiece!

There is only ONE YOU! You ARE a masterpiece! How does it make you feel to know that He designed you to be so very special?

....
....
....
....
....
....
....
....
....
....
....
....

PHOTO CREDIT: SEAD DEDIC

ARE YOU READY?

"Trust in him at all times, you people; pour out
your hearts to him, for God is our refuge."

Psalm 62:8

IN THE DAYS WE ARE NOW LIVING IN, today is a perfect day to trust in the Lord. Allow Him to be your rock. If He is truly your rock, then He will be who you turn to instead of the media or news reports. As you choose to trust Him, fear will fall away. Doubt will disappear. Anxiety will be diminished. Why? Because you are *now* standing in the shadow of the Most High. Trusting Him is what matters most. He *is* and will continue to be the calm in any storm you ever face.

Are you ready?

Write out the words of Matthew 6:33.
Choose to seek Him and trust Him.

PHOTO CREDIT: AZIZ ACHARKI

THE NEW YOU

*"Let your eyes look straight ahead; fix your gaze
directly before you. Give careful thought to the paths
for your feet and be steadfast in all your ways."*

Proverbs 4:25–26

THE *NEW* YOU. Not the former, wounded you ... the one whom family or friends are so accustomed to seeing and hearing from. Here's the deal: Over time, we heal. We grow. And we begin to truly know ourselves better. We know what we like ... and what we don't. We know what helps us soar and what clips our wings. We learn to step into our power and not allow it to be smothered and taken away by others.

A great example was the Apostle Paul, formerly Saul. He was struck down in a moment and then shown the new path he would be on for the rest of his life. His former reputation was one of torturing Christians. He was known to beat and imprison believers and have them killed due to their faith in Jesus. After his conversion, how could others know he had truly changed? He had been widely feared—and *now* he was a changed man. It took *time* for them to see this change in him. It took his confession of faith. It took a changed, contrite heart and dedicating the rest of his life to the very One who had changed him.

And *that* is the key—it takes TIME. It takes FAITH. So, allow yourself time to develop your character, deepen your integrity, and fully know your worth. Allow God's Word to build your confidence in Him.

How do you see yourself? How does God see you according to His Word?

....
....
....
....
....
....
....
....
....
....
....
....
....
....
....
....
....
....
....
....

Love is patient.
Love is kind.
It does not envy
or boast.
It is not proud,
rude, or self-seeking.
It is not easily angry
and keeps no record
of past mistakes.
It does not delight
in evil.
It rejoices in the tur
truth.

BE KIND

"Be kind to one another, tenderhearted, forgiving one another, just as God through Christ has forgiven you."

Ephesians 4:32 (NLT)

I LOVE THIS QUOTE attributed to an unknown author: "After all, it is only when mean people actually are happy and free from suffering that they will stop trying to take us down with them." Now, *that* is a wise thought.

I believe the only way to deal with mean-spirited people is to be kind. For some reason (and only they know why), they are just miserable. Even when you confront them, they have no idea how to respond. These people need love and compassion the most.

Consider King Saul and David. No matter how badly King Saul treated him, David remained pure in heart toward Saul. Even when he had the opportunity to take Saul's life, he did not. May we learn from his example!

Do you have mean-spirited people in your life? Pray for them.
Are you ever mean-spirited? If so, pray a prayer of repentance
and ask God to fill you with compassion and kindness.

BABY STEPS

"But I have calmed and quieted myself, I am like a weaned child with its mother; like a weaned child I am content."

Psalm 131:2

THE VERY THING THAT BREAKS YOU is that which can begin to rebuild you. Your heart can be broken, you can lose your way, you can feel it is all over ... but *something is born* in your soul, and you begin taking baby steps toward healing. You may find that as you stretch out your arms in the darkest moments, you will discover your best friend: YOU.

What is breaking your heart during this season of life?
What newness is being born in your soul today?

....
....
....
....

PHOTO CREDIT: ALEXANDER GREY

REAL

"For you were once darkness, but now you are
light in the Lord. Live as children of light."

Ephesians 5:8

GIVE ME *real.* Every. Single. Time. Those of us who have seen a glimpse of the darkness through depression or anxiety or addiction ... and lived through it ... we know real. We also know the lack of real. We were never called to be perfect during this journey. We've been called to be salt and light. From an Abram to an Abraham. From a Sarai to a Sarah. We have lessons to learn. Maturity in the Spirit waiting to happen. Our journeys toward healing ready to continue.

Are you real? Think deeply about this. Ask God to help you
see clearly who you really are. Don't allow any deception
to shadow who you truly are at the core of you.

PHOTO CREDIT: ERIK MCLEAN

THE POWER OF WORDS

*"Wise words are like deep waters; wisdom flows
from the wise like a bubbling brook."*

Proverbs 18:4 (NLT)

WORDS ARE POWERFUL. We are all human. We fail each other; we fail ourselves. Today, may we be reminded of every word that leaves our mouths. Do they build up? Or tear down? Yes, we have been given that power.

*Write out Psalm 35:28—"My tongue will proclaim your
righteousness, your praises all day long." As you focus
more on Him and grow your character accordingly, your
mouth should also line up. Your words matter!*

PHOTO CREDIT: NICK FEWINGS

WATCH AND LISTEN

"Love is patient and kind. Love is not jealous or boastful or proud or rude. It does not demand its own way. It is not irritable, and it keeps no record of being wronged. It does not rejoice about injustice but rejoices whenever the truth wins out. Love never gives up, never loses faith, is always hopeful, and endures through every circumstance."

1 Corinthians 13:4–7 (NLT)

PEOPLE WILL PROVOKE YOU until they bring out your ugly side, then play the victim when you go there. We've all experienced this. A bully will poke, prod, and provoke. But when you stand up for yourself—well, it's a different story then.

People will show you who they are. Just watch and listen.

Have you had a time of being provoked? Prodded? Bullied? I sure have, and I had to pray for healing and forgiveness. Below,

write about situations or people you might need to forgive.
AND ... learn not to be provoked or to lash out. Instead,
practice praying peace over that person and situation.

PHOTO CREDIT: MATTHEW HENRY

LET YOUR REGRETS GO

"Forget the former things; do not dwell on the past.
See, I am doing a new thing! Now it springs up;
do you not perceive it? I am making a way in the
wilderness and streams in the wasteland."

Isaiah 43:18–19

REGRETS—LET THEM GO. You cannot go back and change the past. Allowing regrets to continue to plague you is counterproductive for your emotional and spiritual health. Walk away and leave those regrets *far behind*.

Then, you can move toward a wonderful future! Pull that heavy bag of regret off your shoulders today.

Do you have regrets in your life that you need to place at the
foot of the Cross? Do that today. Write them down below
or on a separate page, if needed, and LET THEM GO!

PHOTO CREDIT: KYLE GLENN

SURVIVAL

"Now faith is confidence in what we hope for and assurance about what we do not see."

Hebrews 11:1

IF YOU ARE READING THIS, then *you have survived*. Your mother carried you in her womb, and at some point, you entered this world. Place your arms around yourself and give yourself a big hug. Then take a good look in the mirror and remind yourself that you are still living and breathing. And if you are ... there is *hope* for a bright future! There is breath within your lungs to get you from one day to the next. You have survived your best days ... and your worst days.

I encourage you to continue this beautiful path. Set goals for your future and determine just what you want your life to look like. *Look up* and begin asking for what you want in this life. He's listening!

You are a survivor! Write a note to YOU and tell yourself how proud you are to have survived every day up to now! GOD HAS A PLAN FOR YOU!

PHOTO CREDIT: SAKSHAM GANGWAR

WINDS OF CHANGE

"Then Daniel praised the God of heaven and said: 'Praise be to the name of God for ever and ever; wisdom and power are his. He changes times and seasons; he deposes kings and raises up others. He gives wisdom to the wise and knowledge to the discerning. He reveals deep and hidden things; he knows what lies in darkness, and light dwells with him. I thank and praise you, God of my ancestors: You have given me wisdom and power, you have made known to me what we asked of you, you have made known to us the dream of the king.'"

Daniel 2:19–23

I CAN FEEL IT. It's in my soul. Winds of change are coming. Things are not going to stay the way they've always been. There will be crucial changes, necessary changes.

Reality check: Look in the mirror and see the image before you. That person will be with you every day. *That* is a guarantee. The question is whether that person you see is ready for the change that is coming. It's just life. Hearts change. People change. Homes change. Jobs change. The question is: Do you truly want things to stay the way they've always been? That "wheel" in your life that just spins and seemingly goes nowhere?

Listen … truth brings liberation from ties that bind. Truth reveals the darkness in your heart that must be filtered out so new luminosity can expose the way life really should be. Your heart was never meant to be placed within a set of unyielding vise grips. Your heart was created to soar!

I'll leave you with this: All that matters is what truly matters. Where are you? Who are you? Are you living for others, or are you opening your whole heart to what God wants to show you? Life is such an amazing adventure that you surely don't want to be stuck on the side of the road in a ditch. Don't allow roadblocks of bitterness or anger to push you off course. Stay the course and continue your journey toward blue skies that are clear, a heart that is pure, and a mind that is not buried in uncertainty.

Today, feel the winds of change coming and welcome them with open arms. Life will never be the same!

Are you ready for a positive change in your life?

....

....

....

....

....

....

....

....

....

PHOTO CREDIT: UMBERTO GORNI

SAFE HARBOR

"Then they cried out to the Lord in their trouble,
and he delivered them from their distress."

Psalm 107:6

TRAUMA HAPPENS. The most hurtful part of trauma is when our story is misaligned, not trusted, or not believed. May we all have a safe harbor in the presence of those who will honor our vulnerability and resilience to heal.

In time, we do heal. *You* will heal. Having a strong support system in place is vital to helping you along your healing journey.

Do you have a support system in place? There are so
many wonderful resources for support, including
family, friends, support groups, and church groups—
even Facebook has avenues for emotional and spiritual
support. And God is ultimately your safe harbor!

PHOTO CREDIT: VICTOR RODVANG

THE GRAND PERFORMANCE

Thank You, Father,
That the greatest victories I've seen
Have come out of struggles fought
Within my own heart
When there's just You and me.
Deliverance performed by Your Almighty Hand
When there's no parting of waters
Or great speeches or applause
Just the quietness of You moving
Within the depths of my heart ...
That part placed within me
That continues to seek
A little peace, a little calm
A little joy and a little balance.
Thank You, Father,
That You are quietly molding me
By a Grand Performance
Wrought by Your Loving Hands
With a Heavenly Promise
That You will be faithful to complete
What You first began.

What victories have you seen rise out of the ashes of your struggles?

PHOTO CREDIT: MARINA VITALE

LIFT MY EYES

"I look up to the mountains—does my help come from there?
My help comes from the Lord, who made heaven and earth!"

Psalm 121:1–2 (NLT)

FROM MY JOURNAL

Every single day I am growing stronger
The blood pumps through this strong heart within me
It has carried me through so many things
And I know it will not fail me now
I lift my eyes to the Heavens
As I feel the strength and power underneath me
Surrounding me with the many gifts I have been given
This woman knows who she is
And she knows she'll never lose herself again.

Think about it: "She'll never lose herself again."
What do these words mean to you?

PHOTO CREDIT: LLOYD NEWMAN

SEE BEYOND THE NATURAL

*"For God so loved the world that He gave His
only begotten Son, that whoever believes in Him
should not perish but have everlasting life."*

John 3:16 (NKJV)

FOR AS LONG AS I CAN REMEMBER, I have walked into
places and seen souls. Every single person has one. And each person has a heart.
If we knew their story ... if they knew ours ... things in this world would be
much different.

May we always have eyes that see beyond the natural. Beyond the outer
layer that surrounds those around us. May we hear beyond the words they
speak and know that there is a soul deep inside of them wanting to be heard
and understood.

"If only our eyes saw souls instead of bodies, how
different our ideas of beauty would be."

Allow your eyes to begin seeing others' spiritual need for

Jesus. Begin praying for your family and friends to truly know Him. Make a list of those you feel burdened for. Begin praying for each one today. As you are healing, you can see God begin to move in their lives.

....
....
....
....
....
....
....
....
....
....
....
....
....
....
....
....
....
....
....
....
....
....
....
....
....

PHOTO CREDIT: SHERRY STAKER COVER

WELCOME PEACE

"'For I know the plans I have for you,' declares the Lord,
'plans to prosper you and not to harm you, plans to
give you hope and a future. Then you will call on
me and come and pray to me, and I will listen to
you. You will seek me and find me when you seek me
with all your heart. I will be found by you,' declares
the Lord, 'and will bring you back from captivity.'"

Jeremiah 29:11–14

THIS VERSE IS SO IMPORTANT—especially for those of us who have experienced trauma. Choose peace. Pray. Remember that anxiety is a fear of the future. Only He holds the future in His very capable hands. We can trust this truth. This verse is a promise to cling to every day.

Write out Jeremiah 29:11-14 below. Thank God for
having your future in His very capable hands.

WELCOME PEACE

PHOTO CREDIT: DALTON SMITH

THE MEANING AND PURPOSE OF LIFE

"The meaning of life is to find your gift.
The purpose of life is to give it away."

David Viscott

THAT QUOTE HAS BEEN WIDELY SHARED in various forms and is often attributed to the likes of William Shakespeare and Pablo Picasso, but it was first penned by an author named David Viscott in 1993. It's a powerful message that will continue to resonate with generations.

Think about the words. And then—don't you dare keep your gifts to yourself! You have arms—**HUG** those who need it. You have lips—**SPEAK** positive words over yourself and those around you. You have a heart—**LOVE** with everything that is within you.

Are you ready to BE love? To accept love? To receive love?

PHOTO CREDIT: MICHAEL KURZYNOWSKI

SITTING ON THE DOCK

*"That is why I tell you not to worry about everyday life—
whether you have enough food and drink, or enough clothes
to wear. Isn't life more than food, and your body more than
clothing? Look at the birds. They don't plant or harvest or
store food in barns, for your heavenly Father feeds them.
And aren't you far more valuable to him than they are?
Can all your worries add a single moment to your life?"*

Matthew 6:25–27 (NLT)

LYING IN A HAMMOCK, looking out over the ocean, I noticed the seagulls hovering over the beach and landing on the dock in front of me. I watched as they fluttered around, seeming to communicate with one another and then calm themselves as they each found a little place to perch at the end of the dock. They were completely still and so peaceful.

I watched them, taking in the sun and the cool morning breeze, and I noticed they were worried about absolutely nothing ... *nada*. Oh, to be a seagull in Cozumel! What a beautiful place to be—surrounded by the most stunning azure water, the beaming sunshine that seems never-ending, and all the peace they could possibly want. They weren't worried about the weather, their food, their job, their home, their relationships, or their finances! They were just sitting peacefully in all of God's magnificent glory in Cozumel, Mexico.

Lord, remind us that there are no worries to hold within us. Just a place at the dock of our "bay" to place our fullest trust in You, acknowledging that if You take care of these lovely seagulls every day, You will certainly prove Yourself faithful in our lives. You are Jehovah-Jireh, the God who provides. Thank You for the reminder in Your Word of how deeply You care for us, find great value in us, and desire that we will trust You in all things. Amen.

What worries do you need to place at the foot of the Cross today?

. . . .

. . . .

. . . .

. . . .

. . . .

. . . .

. . . .

. . . .

. . . .

. . . .

. . . .

. . . .

. . . .

. . . .

PHOTO CREDIT: JOHN JENNINGS

CREATIVE MESSAGES

"There is no one holy like the Lord; there is no one besides you; there is no Rock like our God."

1 Samuel 2:2

Oh, Lord God, you are quite amazing. My heart is so grateful for the words of wisdom that You send—just the right words at the right time. What a blessing to see eyes "get it" as their hearts begin to open. The creative messages You share help precious people to choose life, extend forgiveness, and grab hold of a lifeline called hope—they see how to finally let go of things they have held on to for years.

Yes, I am so very grateful for Your words and for You being everything that You are.

Jot down a love letter to Him today ... right where you are.

PHOTO CREDIT: JAMIE STREET

TRUE NORTH

"O Lord, you have examined my heart and know everything about me. You know when I sit down or stand up. You know my thoughts even when I'm far away. You see me when I travel and when I rest at home. You know everything I do. You know what I am going to say even before I say it, Lord. You go before me and follow me. You place your hand of blessing on my head. Such knowledge is too wonderful for me, too great for me to understand!"

Psalm 139:1–6 (NLT)

WHAT IS YOUR *true north*? It's that place in the deepest part of you that nurtures your soul. It's that voice that whispers, *You CAN do this.* Your *true north* is that simple knowing that you are stronger than you think and you are more valuable than you feel; it's a calling within you that guides you to another day.

Every single day, we can choose to trust that voice. We can choose to be a kinder person and a more loving human being, and we can choose to allow our hearts to be nurtured instead of sabotaged. *Choose you.*

Where is your true north? What nurtures your soul? Below, write your favorite Scripture or the one at the top of this devotion.

PHOTO CREDIT: MARLENA COMPSTON

NOT-ENOUGHNESS

"Look to the Lord and his strength; seek his face always."

1 Chronicles 16:11

NOT-ENOUGHNESS—that concept needs to be expired from your mental vocabulary. It's that language within your own heart that screams, "YOU ARE NOT ENOUGH—YOU ARE A FAILURE." NO ma'am! NO sir! You take charge and remove the voice that tries to deplete your power. YOU ARE ENOUGH ... AND HAVE ALWAYS BEEN.

Write: I AM ENOUGH. IN HIM, I HAVE ALWAYS BEEN ENOUGH. You are! Begin today to embrace how special you are. NO ONE is just like you, dear friend.

....

....

....

....

PHOTO CREDIT: JARED SUBIA

SHARE YOUR CROWN

"Praise the Lord, my soul; all my inmost being, praise his holy name. Praise the Lord, my soul, and forget not all his benefits—who forgives all your sins and heals all your diseases, who redeems your life from the pit and crowns you with love and compassion, who satisfies your desires with good things so that your youth is renewed like the eagle's."

Psalm 103:1–5

THE SPIRIT SHOWED ME something so clearly: We, as brothers or sisters in Christ—and especially as women—should always be willing to share our crowns. We should always want our friends to win. We should be willing to step up and care for them. Sometimes, that means a meal, a phone call, an offer to visit, or a hand to hold, and certainly being a friend with whom to pray.

Sharing our crowns means we have a deep awareness that others are worthy and deserving of love, care, and understanding from us. There is no time for nonsense or drama.

We share compassion because He has already extended it to us—and we know, without a shadow of a doubt, that we would be nothing without Him. The anointing … HIS anointing … is so very important.

In the end, we will receive crowns in Heaven to reward us for a life well-lived. Those same glorious crowns we are given will then be cast at His feet.

When you fully embrace the beautiful person God created you to be, you will have opportunities to share your crown. This can include your testimony … your own story of defeat and redemption, of sharing your heart with others and pointing them to Him. Begin embracing *your* crown today! Do you see it? Is the picture becoming clearer for you?

Can you think of a time when a friend shared her crown by making you feel special, cared for, and valued? Embark on your own journey to be "that" woman who is always willing to share her crown.

....

....

....

....

....

....

....

....

....

....

....

....

....

....

PHOTO CREDIT: JELLEKE VANOOTEGHEM

PRAY. SEEK. LISTEN.

"Stay away from a fool, for you will not find knowledge on their lips. The wisdom of the prudent is to give thought to their ways, but the folly of fools is deception."

Proverbs 14:7–8

WE CAN TRULY APPRECIATE and love the fact that Jesus is savvy. Discerning. Well-meaning. He wants all of us to win. He forgives. He saves. He protects. He provides. He listens.

But while He was on this Earth, He confronted deception. He confronted the arrogant with their arrogance. He questioned the prideful regarding their pride, and He shot straight to the dark hearts of the religious Pharisees. In Matthew 23:13, the Lord said to them, "Woe to you, teachers of the law and Pharisees, you hypocrites! You shut the door of the kingdom of heaven in people's faces. You yourselves do not enter, nor will you let those enter who are trying to."

Jesus spoke *truth*. He invited those who believed in Him to follow Him. His every move was for His Father—*our Father*—with eternity always on His mind. Your eternity. My eternity. Every word spoken from His lips embraced the entirety of humanity. Ultimately, He gave us the only answer we will ever need: Himself.

May we be in the Word so we can *know* the will of God and the words of God. May we pray continually and ask Him to show us when to open a door and when to shut it. These words beg me to enter my prayer closet and ask God to show me much more wisdom in this area.

Do we continue to tolerate rude, hurtful, and harsh behavior? Once such a person clearly shows us who they are, we should shake the dust off our feet and move on, as Scripture states in the New Testament (see Matthew 10:14–16).

Pray. Seek. Listen. Repeat. Answers *will* come.

How does this devotion speak to you in your own circumstances?

....

....

....

....

....

....

....

....

....

....

....

....

....

....

....

....

PHOTO CREDIT: HUGUES DE BUYER-MIMEURE

HIS PEACE

"Be anxious for nothing, but in everything by prayer and supplication, with thanksgiving, let your requests be made known to God; and the peace of God, which surpasses all understanding, will guard your hearts and minds through Christ Jesus."

Philippians 4:6–7 (NKJV)

I'M FINDING THAT THE OLDER I GET, the easier it is to trust in Him. I don't have to stress over every detail. Why? First, because things have a way of working out. Second, and more importantly, He is omnipresent, omnipotent, and omniscient.

How comforting that should be to us! If we trust Him, we won't be anxious. Anxiety is the fear of the future. The Holy Spirit revealed that to me many years ago. Everything is a *process*! Don't beat yourself up if you experience anxiety.

I encourage you to begin trusting Him more. *Pray.* Journal. Tell Him how you feel. Are you angry? Tell him. Write it out. Are you grateful? Share it. Are you believing that your prayers will be answered? Trust Him with every detail. He cares deeply for every detail of your life. He wants you to experience His peace.

Look up the definitions for the words omnipresent, omnipotent, *and* omniscient. *How comforting it is to know that He is always, always here for you. He will never leave you.*

PHOTO CREDIT: ALEKSANDRA SAPOZHNIKOVA

ASPIRE TO INSPIRE

*"And don't forget to do good and to share with those
in need. These are the sacrifices that please God."*

Hebrews 13:16 (NLT)

IT'S NOT JUST ABOUT US, you know?

It's about leading others to freedom when they're surrounded by darkness.

Caring for someone and expecting nothing in return.

Holding their hand and praying for them when they feel all is lost.

Pointing them to hope. Helping them to breathe again.

Only LOVE from above can truly heal us. Cleanse us. Forgive us.

Give us everlasting hope and joy.

May we aspire to inspire.

*Do you naturally help others as you see their physical, spiritual, or
emotional needs? It feels so good to help others. God truly blesses
us as we get our eyes off ourselves and on to those around us.*

PHOTO CREDIT: KATHY LAMB

THE NARROW GATE

*"Enter through the narrow gate. For wide is
the gate and broad is the road that leads to
destruction, and many enter through it."*

Matthew 7:13

LIFE OFFERS MANY PATHS. Some are born into wealth, power, and influence. Others simply are not. Those born into wealth, power, and influence may lead, but they also may struggle with greed, addiction, control, pride, or having faith. Those born with less might also struggle. These people may carry heavy resentments and jealousy in their hearts, always asking why they were cursed in this life.

It's interesting to think of which person would bend his knee first. The prideful, rich person who is at the end of their rope, or the broke person who hates the whole world, including himself?

Are you one of them? Or are you somewhere in between, just looking for direction? God wants you WHOLE, HEALED, and entering through the narrow gate.

....
....
....
....
....
....
....
....
....
....
....
....
....
....
....
....
....
....
....
....
....
....

PHOTO CREDIT: NADHIL RAMANDHA

NO ROOM

*"Make every effort to live in peace with
everyone and to be holy."*

Hebrews 12:14

THERE IS NO ROOM for selfishness. There is absolutely no room, no time, for jealousy. Quarrels must cease. Strife must end. Listen to the stirring of the Holy Ghost! There is plenty of room for healing.

Let us make even more space to usher in the anointing of the Holy Spirit. Why, you ask? Because millions of people need hope, healing, and salvation.

*If you are stuck in quarreling, jealousy, strife, or anything
else that disrupts your peace, lay it down right here.*

....
....
....
....

PHOTO CREDIT: MARLENA COMPSTON

TEACH OUR CHILDREN

"If we confess our sins, he is faithful and just and will
forgive us our sins and purify us from all unrighteousness."

1 John 1:9

WHEN MY CHILDREN WERE YOUNG, after tucking them in bed, I taught them this Scripture. It was the sweetest thing to hear their little voices recite those words. They are now grown. I sure miss those days.

We have such a tremendous responsibility and blessing to teach our children about Jesus.

If you have children, I encourage you to teach them Scripture. If
you are praying to be a parent, TRUST Him with your situation.

TEACH OUR CHILDREN

PHOTO CREDIT: NINE KOEPFER

PURE IN HEART

"Blessed are the pure in heart, for they will see God."

Matthew 5:8

PURE IN HEART: No ill motives. No selfish ambition. Choosing to live transparently. No deception. No cover-ups. A determination to be passionate about caring for others. Having a heart that always wants the best for others. I choose *this*.

Remember the truth that we are all in different seasons. Some of us are lost. Some of us are "found" but still wandering in the desert. Some of us are growing in our faith. For all of us, living water is right in front of us. God is pouring out His grace to each one of us ... if we will *just choose Him*.

As I was writing tonight, I looked up the phrase *pure in heart*. An article by Got Questions Ministries gave me some excellent additional insights:

"Being pure in heart involves having a singleness of heart toward God. A pure heart has no hypocrisy, no guile, no hidden motives. The pure heart is marked by transparency and an uncompromising desire to please God in all things. It is more than an external purity of behavior; it is an *internal* purity of soul."

The only way we can be pure in heart is to give our lives to Jesus and ask Him to do the cleansing work. Psalm 51:10 says, "Create in me a pure heart, O God, and renew a steadfast spirit within me." God is the One who makes our hearts pure—by the sacrifice of His Son and through His sanctifying work in our lives (see also 1 John 3:1–3)."[2]

Choose HIM. It's so very simple. Write about what "pure in heart" means to you.

....
....
....
....
....
....
....
....
....
....
....
....
....
....
....
....
....
....
....
....

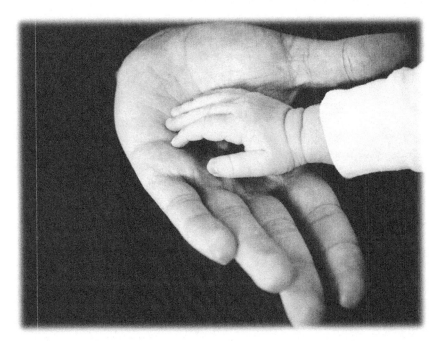

PHOTO CREDIT: LIANE METZLER

THE GOOD STUFF

"Because your love is better than life,
my lips will glorify you."

Psalm 63:3

Trust Him.

Depend on Him.

Praise Him.

Talk to Him.

Find strength in Him.

Lean into Him.

Write your own short declaration of trusting Him below.

PHOTO CREDIT: DAVE RUCK

LIVE IN PEACE

*"Above all, love each other deeply, because
love covers over a multitude of sins."*

1 Peter 4:8

DON'T LIVE YOUR LIFE to make other people miserable. The
"make you pay because you did something that made me unhappy" days need
to GO! Everyone messes up at some point. Everyone deserves some grace ...
including *you*!

Now, go patch up your relationships and live in peace!

*With whom do you need to make peace? Ask God to show you open
doors for reconciliation. You will know when the time is right.*

....

....

....

....

PHOTO CREDIT: ALEX SHUTE

GRACE...BEAUTIFUL GRACE

"However, I consider my life worth nothing to me; my only aim is to finish the race and complete the task the Lord Jesus has given me—the task of testifying to the good news of God's grace."

Acts 20:24

GRACE. I woke up this morning to this one beautiful word. A new day to extend grace to myself and those around me. It's easy to hold a grudge against someone, to determine not to spend time with them, or even to choose to punish them by your silence. Let's determine to extend grace today.

Here are some ways to begin:

* **Start with you.** Yes, *you* deserve some grace, too.

* **Just let go.** Quit carrying all that baggage around your shoulders.

* **Live in gratitude.** You have so much to be grateful for.

* **Forgive.** Forgive. Forgive.

* **Apologize where needed.** Don't hold on to your pride. Why do you even do that?

* **Be mindful of others.** It's not all about you. There's a whole world that needs grace extended.

* **Speak kindly.** Make every attempt to hold your tongue. The book of James has much wisdom on this subject.

* **Have compassion.** We all need this. Extend compassion. It's not that difficult to do.

* **Accept people for who they are.** This might be a tough one for you. We are all on a journey; some of us are more enlightened than others. Some are not enlightened at all. Can you love them anyway ... right where they are?

Extend grace today. Look in the mirror and start right there!

Write the bullet points in bold above. Personalize each point.

....

....

....

....

....

....

....

....

....

....

....

....

....

....

....

....

....

PHOTO CREDIT: ALLEF VINICIUS

EXPECTATIONS

"For My thoughts are not your thoughts, nor
are your ways My ways,' says the Lord.
'For as the heavens are higher than the earth,
So are My ways higher than your ways, And
My thoughts than your thoughts.'"

Isaiah 55:8–9 (NKJV)

I'VE BEEN DOING A LOT of reflecting on the word *expectations*. Anytime we feel upset or angry, we might need to take a step back. I've done this myself recently. Let's consider our expectations and whether something happened the way we had hoped. We expect "this" or "that" to work out a certain way. If our expectations are not met, it can cause feelings of upset or even anger.

Join me in praying this simple prayer: "Lord God, I place my expectations into Your willing and capable hands, knowing that You care for me. That you are guiding me. And that, above all, You are gently guiding me down the right path, even when I cannot see where it leads."

And remember, Abraham had no idea where he was going when he was sent … *but* he trusted God's hand to place him at the right place. And certainly, at the right time.

Do you get upset when your expectations are not met? How do you handle that situation?

EXPECTATIONS

PHOTO CREDIT: BEN WHITE

PRAY

*But to you who are listening I say: Love your
enemies, do good to those who hate you, bless those
who curse you, pray for those who mistreat you.*

Luke 6:27–28

PRAY FOR DISCERNMENT. Even Jesus had a traitor in his circle
of friends. One huge difference, when you have power from the Holy Spirit, is
not to push traitors out of your life. Pray diligently for those who betray you.
Pray they will find their identity in Christ. Pray for their wounded hearts to
be healed and whole.

The Word says it's easy to love those who love us. It's much harder to love
those who don't. Luke 6:27–36 is a great read on this topic.

Are there people in your life who are difficult to love?

PHOTO CREDIT: MELISSA ASKEW

LOVE ONE ANOTHER

"To love him with all your heart, with all your understanding and with all your strength, and to love your neighbor as yourself is more important than all burnt offerings and sacrifices."

Mark 12:33

I WILL NEVER, ever stop reaching out to others. You have no idea if someone is about to give up. Allow compassion to rise in your heart. Reach out beyond yourself to give hope to someone who feels hopeless.

Don't hate anyone.

Don't wish to see someone fail.

Don't wish to see someone hurt.

Don't wish to see someone broken.

Don't wish to see someone face tragedy.

Just don't.

Love one another.

How does this speak to you?

PHOTO CREDIT: SLAV ROMANOV

TRUE PURPOSE

"For you created my inmost being; you knit me together in my mother's womb.

I praise you because I am fearfully and wonderfully made; your works are wonderful, I know that full well. My frame was not hidden from you when I was made in the secret place, when I was woven together in the depths of the earth. Your eyes saw my unformed body; all the days ordained for me were written in your book before one of them came to be. How precious to me are your thoughts, God! How vast is the sum of them! Were I to count them, they would outnumber the grains of sand – when I awake, I am still with you."

Psalm 139:13–18

MAY WE UNDERSTAND who we are and why we were created:
in His image
for fellowship
to serve others
to be salt and light

to embrace that we are *exactly* the way we were meant to be

Once we understand our true purpose, there won't be time to dislike the person we see in the mirror.

Who are you, friend? What do you feel your true purpose is?

PHOTO CREDIT: DEWANG GUPTA

TOTALLY TRANSFORMED

*"Jesus stopped and called them. 'What do you want
me to do for you?' he asked.*

*'Lord,' they answered, 'we want our sight.' Jesus had
compassion on them and touched their eyes. Immediately
they received their sight and followed Him."*

Matthew 20:32–34

THESE FIVE POWERFUL WORDS say so much: "Lord, we
want our sight."

Jesus knew what these men wanted before He even asked them. He wanted
to hear their heart's desire. Two blind men acknowledged His power by calling
Him "Lord" and then had the faith to ask for their sight.

Jesus was moved with compassion by their requests and their faith. He
didn't ask what they could do for Him. He didn't require them to get their
lives straightened out first. He didn't ask them what church they attended. He
didn't ask them for anything. He simply touched their eyes. And it changed
them. These two men gained their eyesight that very day. They also gained
spiritual eyes ... and then chose to follow the very One who had the power to
heal and save them from their former darkness.

Thank You, Father, for Your ability and desire to totally transform our lives from the inside out. Like a butterfly, we were in a cocoon, and You want to set us free.

What do you want to ask God to do for you today?

....
....
....
....
....
....
....
....
....
....
....
....
....
....
....
....
....
....
....

PHOTO CREDIT: FRANK MCKENNA

AN ORPHAN'S HEART

""If you love me, obey my commandments. And I will ask the Father, and he will give you another Advocate, who will never leave you. He is the Holy Spirit, who leads into all truth. The world cannot receive him, because it isn't looking for him and doesn't recognize him. But you know him, because he lives with you now and later will be in you. No, I will not abandon you as orphans—I will come to you. Soon the world will no longer see me, but you will see me. Since I live, you also will live."

John 14:15–19 (NLT)

DO YOU HAVE an orphan's heart? One that never feels at home? A heart that longs for a place of peace and belonging to call your very own?

You do not have to live life out of an empty place within you. God is so willing to heal every hurt. Every wound. Every scar. Draw close to Him. He will never leave you. He will never turn you away.

Let's talk about this. Have you felt that you didn't belong?

PHOTO CREDIT: MARLENA COMPSTON

THE COLOR OF OUR SKIN

"Don't just pretend to love others. Really love them. Hate what is wrong. Hold tightly to what is good. Love each other with genuine affection, and take delight in honoring each other."

Romans 12:9–10 (NLT)

LET'S SHED A LITTLE LIGHT on what might be a touchy subject. If you see skin color or ethnicity before you see a human being with a heart, soul, and spirit, may I suggest some time on your knees in prayer? Ask for judgment or hatred to be removed from your heart and replaced with compassion for all human beings.

Please always remember—we *all* bleed the same color.

Have you ever had a prejudiced heart? Many times, this is passed on from generation to generation. If so, ask God to break up those generational prejudices. Ask Him to

allow you to see others through His eyes. And remember that He created every single one of our beating hearts.

PHOTO CREDIT: EYASU ETSUB

"REMEMBER MY CHAINS"

"I, Paul, write this greeting in my own hand.
Remember my chains. Grace be with you."

Colossians 4:18

AS I WAS READING this chapter in Colossians, this verse stood out to me. I thought about Paul, sitting in prison and writing to his friends in the church. In his own way ... and in his own words ... Paul asked for prayer by saying, "Remember my chains." The chains Paul spoke of were probably around his feet. In closing his letter, he asked his friends not to forget him. To pray for him. The words He chose are very touching: "Remember my chains."

What chains do you need to be removed in your life? Jesus can. Jesus will. Just ask. He's waiting to hear your voice.

Where are you tonight in your heart and in your head? What chains are around you?

PHOTO CREDIT: DINO REICHMUTH

THE JOURNEY

*"So be strong and courageous! Do not be afraid and do not
panic before them. For the Lord your God will personally
go ahead of you. He will neither fail you nor abandon you."*

Deuteronomy 31:6 (NLT)

I SO LOVE THE WAY God moves in our lives. The journey doesn't
always make sense, but somehow, He works things out for our best and His
glory. I believe my part in this journey, down all the pathways, whether smooth
or bumpy, is to learn to trust His heart and listen for His voice and His gentle,
unwavering guidance and direction.

I'm so grateful for a Heavenly Father who never forgets me or abandons
my heart.

*How is God moving in your life? What Scriptures
have spoken to your heart recently?*

PHOTO CREDIT: AMY TREASURE

CHOOSE PEACE

*"Peace I leave with you; my peace I give you. I do
not give to you as the world gives. Do not let your
hearts be troubled and do not be afraid."*

John 14:27

TODAY, YOUR THOUGHTS don't get to sabotage you! You
know—those thoughts that never end and keep you on a "merry-go-round"
of craziness. Listen to this! *YOU* can control your thoughts. *YOU* have been
given a great mind! *YOU* have the power ... take that power today! *YOU*
determine where, when, and why these thoughts happen.

Choose peace every day—because it is simply yours for the taking.

***Do you have peace today? Write out John
14:27 and then memorize it.***

PHOTO CREDIT: CHRIS LAWTON

LOCATION, LOCATION, LOCATION

"You will keep in perfect peace those whose minds are steadfast, because they trust in you."

Isaiah 26:3

YOUR REAL ESTATE TODAY is ... PEACE. When anything else presents itself—worry, fear, sickness, or hopelessness—push them aside and step into the power of the Holy Spirit.

God *is* with us. Read His Word. Long to know Him. Seek healing. Desire to heal from your past. *You no longer live there.* Your real estate is right where you stand today ... and *you are worth it.*

Where is your real estate today? Are you located in peace or turmoil? Harmony or anxiety? Be honest with yourself. Now write how you would like your life to be transformed. What steps can you take for that to happen?

PHOTO CREDIT: GASTON ROULSTONE

BROKEN WINGS

"Cast all your anxiety on him because he cares for you."

1 Peter 5:7

SO MANY ARE GOING THROUGH heartbreak lately. It's been on my mind that we all experience broken wings. Those times when we simply cannot breathe deeply. Those moments when we would rather be swept away in slumber and not think. When our thoughts are heavy like black, sticky tar. When our arms feel heavy. Remember, though, these moments do not last.

The sun will rise tomorrow. The moon will surely be in the sky. Your heart *will* feel lighter. Though not today, it will sing again. Those moments of the light breeze blowing through your hair ... when the birds are singing and you awaken from your sorrowful sleep to a brighter, golden day.

Healing is coming. You will feel whole again. Your broken wings, love, will mend with time. Now sleep peacefully, knowing there is a Heavenly Father above who is watching over you.

Are your wings broken? Only He can mend you the way you need to be mended. Make this a prayer and ask to be whole and healed.

PHOTO CREDIT: LENA POLISHKO

SEASON OF WINTER

"Let us acknowledge the Lord; let us press on to acknowledge him. As surely as the sun rises, he will appear; he will come to us like the winter rains, like the spring rains that water the earth."

Hosea 6:3

WINTER BRINGS A CHILLING FREEZe right into our bones. Soft layers of snow fall and blanket the world as we know it. During winter, there are places of darkness; a stillness lurks, making everything appear dormant and lifeless and lonely.

But underneath this snowy, white blanket are tender flowers being prepared to burst forth with new life ... at just the right time. Preparations have started. Spring will bring new growth and beginnings. One door closed ... and a new door opened. We will experience new life. We will feel the warmth as the sunshine returns from hiding, touching all the frozen places.

The warmth will melt away the cobwebs of darkness, the emptiness of the season, and will welcome us into this new space and new place. Exiting the former darkness, spring bursts forth! A new time to bloom and to feel whole; a special time for everything to be beautiful again.

May we learn to find peace in winter, knowing that spring is coming. A promise that it is never late ... but always right on time.

What are some of your favorite memories of winter, or snow, or being in a place that feels that way? Is the season you are in full of fulfillment, or do you feel empty right now?

PHOTO CREDIT: KATERINA KERDI

THE REST OF THE STORY

"Jesus answered, 'I am the way and the truth and the life. No one comes to the Father except through me.'"

John 14:6

WHY DO WE LEARN MORE in the desert than we do on the mountaintop? Let's consider Peter. Jesus clearly told Peter that Peter would deny Him three times, but Peter couldn't even imagine denying his Lord. Test day came, though, and Peter failed miserably.

Imagine the moments and the days *after* Peter's denial. I've always envisioned Peter in a soggy, dreary alley surrounded by and wrapped in cloaks of darkness, feeling completely devastated and destroyed inside. I imagine him carrying huge boulders of guilt on his shoulders. Certainly, this caused his head to hang and his heart to sink in complete shame and agony. The very One who loved him so dearly ... Peter had denied even knowing. Peter's value was depleted, and he was emptied of himself. This is a sobering statement.

But **the rest of the story** goes like this: Jesus restored Peter.

Then, out of darkness came a bright light as Peter was completely restored by our Lord Jesus Christ. Soon after, Peter preached and led three thousand souls to salvation in *one day*. Praise God! Praise our Healing God, our Faithful Father.

Another great example is the Prophet Elijah. In 1 Kings 19, we can follow a very interesting timeline as Elijah experiences a great victory only to find himself running for his life, falling beneath a tree, and telling the Lord he is ready to give up ... and to *now* just let him die. Haven't some of us found ourselves in that darkness?

The Lord had a *much better* plan than Elijah did. The Lord sent provisions of food and water through an angel for Elijah to eat and drink. He then instructed Elijah to rest. *After* Elijah did what the Lord told him to do (a lesson in itself), Elijah then traveled to Mount Horeb. Note that the meaning of *Horeb* is "to be in ruins, lay in waste."

The Lord asked Elijah what he was doing. Elijah stated that he had been zealous for the Lord and the others were not—DO YOU SEE IT? Possibly Elijah was feeling like God had *forgotten* him in his well-doing. He wanted to remind God that his heart was toward Him. Notice how the Lord instructs Elijah to find Him.

"The Lord said, 'Go out and stand on the mountain in the presence of the Lord, for the Lord is about to pass by.' Then a great and powerful wind tore the mountains apart and shattered the rocks before the Lord, but the Lord was not in the wind. After the wind there was an earthquake, but the Lord was not in the earthquake. After the earthquake came a fire, but the Lord was not in the fire. And after the fire came a gentle whisper. When Elijah heard it, he pulled his cloak over his face and went out and stood at the mouth of the cave" (1 Kings 19:11–13).

Elijah needed to find the Lord again. Think about it ... Elijah, a great prophet of God, ran away in fear when Jezebel threatened his life. Now God was instructing him to *go out and stand*. Elijah was restored as the Lord gave him instructions on his next journey. Eventually, Elijah was taken up into the clouds in a chariot. AMAZING!

Testing will come, and we might fail miserably, but this prepares us for the next test. Failing gives us an even greater opportunity for future success. It's true: Disappointment may happen. Discouragement may cause us to fall, but **the rest of the story** is that there is always a new day, and restoration is just around the corner.

Don't give up! His mercies are *new* every single morning. Place all your disappointments at the foot of the Cross. Lay your discouragement down. You don't have to carry it. You ALSO have a *rest of the story*, so be encouraged, and listen for that still, small voice to speak to your heart once again.

How does this devotion speak to you regarding your life?

PHOTO CREDIT: GIULIA BERTELLI

THE HEART'S CHOICE

"And do not grieve the Holy Spirit of God, with whom you were sealed for the day of redemption. Get rid of all bitterness, rage and anger, brawling and slander, along with every form of malice. Be kind and compassionate to one another, forgiving each other, just as in Christ God forgave you."

Ephesians 4:30–32

UNFORGIVENESS IS THE ISSUE that my precious Savior has been "whittling away" from the deepest chambers of my heart. I am learning, in this season of my life, that choosing to hold on to unforgiveness is nothing less than me deciding to be bitter toward those who have hurt me. In the span of our lives, we've all had varying degrees of pain inflicted in ways that cause us to become overprotective of our hearts. When we have been hurt, we build an invisible wall of protection around us that says, "I will never let anyone hurt me like that again." What we might not realize is that when we choose to say, "Never again," we are placing ourselves into a transparent prison that binds up the power God freely gives us to extend forgiveness to others.

Over the past several years, the Lord has continued to deal with me on this subject. He has lovingly drawn me to Matthew 18 and the deeply indebted servant. This servant was graciously extended forgiveness by his master, only for that same forgiven servant to come against someone else who owed him a much smaller debt. How many times I have been guilty of being like that unforgiving servant with my own grip around someone's throat, demanding immediate payment for my pain.

According to the Word, this servant was handed over to be tortured until he paid back all that he owed. The servant's decision to hold on to his unforgiveness cost him dearly. We read in Matthew 18:22 that Jesus said we are to forgive (get this!) seventy TIMES seven. Does this mean that God does not allow us to fall short of what He requires? Is it possible that He allows us times of adversity before we get to the other side of such sins as unforgiveness? I do believe He allows us to "wallow" in the muck just as the prodigal son did. Remember, in the middle of the prodigal's "wallowing," it became very clear to him that something had to change and that change had to begin with himself. Maybe this is the exact time head knowledge finally becomes heart knowledge!

I'm so thankful we serve a *loving, very patient* Heavenly Father who desires His children to be healed, restored, and whole!

Yes ... God is giving me a clear vision of my Savior hanging painfully from the Cross of Calvary as He prayed, "Forgive them, for they do not know what they are doing" (Luke 23:34). Can you see it? God gave His perfect heavenly example through the gift of Jesus of not only forgiveness but also meekness. Those unforgiving souls standing at the foot of the Cross were the epitome of ugliness as they spit their curses at the One who could be their life's greatest blessing.

Unforgiveness is ugly baggage to carry around. It can cause our countenance to change and, without a doubt, completely steal our joy. Unforgiveness can also be compared to an emotional malignant cancer that feeds off the bitterness we clutch so tightly within us. The longer we choose to hold on to it, the more miserable we are.

Our Heavenly Father never created us to carry all these burdens. He wants us to lean on Him and develop a deeper trust in Him so we may know how to "cast our cares on Him" (I Peter 5:7). God's desire is for us to repent, *without delay*, when we feel the claws of bitterness taking root in our heart. What a revelation that we can choose to walk in His power and extend forgiveness to those who have wounded us!

Oh, Lord, may I never again make a choice to hold unforgiveness in my heart. Help me, Father, to always understand that You didn't have to forgive those at Calvary; You chose to! In that same vein, if I make forgiveness a choice of my heart, You will always honor that choice.

God freely gives us the power to extend forgiveness to others as forgiveness has been extended to us through His Son, our Savior. How grateful we can be that God loves us too much to leave us where we are!

What bitterness do you hold in your heart? Are you ready to let it go?

....

....

....

....

....

....

....

....

....

....

PHOTO CREDIT: JOSE' PINTO

TIMING IS EVERYTHING

"God has made everything beautiful for its own time.
He has planted eternity in the human heart, but even
so, people cannot see the whole scope of God's work
from beginning to end. So I concluded there is nothing
better than to be happy and enjoy ourselves as long as
we can. And people should eat and drink and enjoy the
fruits of their labor, for these are gifts from God."

Ecclesiastes 3:11–13 (NLT)

IT'S 5 A.M., and Scripture is swirling in my head. I've been meditating on Ecclesiastes the past few days and the way God has this beautiful, amazing way of speaking to us. He loves us when we're close, and He loves us when we're distant, too, and going about the busyness of our lives.

Timing is everything, and He has made a special way to communicate with us through His Word. How practical these words in the first chapter of Ecclesiastes are—and some of my very favorite words to cling to: "He has planted eternity in the human heart" (verse 11).

No matter where we are today, we have a future to place in His capable, loving hands. No matter the hurt we have endured, we can be assured that He has a way of healing every wound. No matter the words that have caused pain,

He has a way of breathing words of life into our spirit. With our successes, we can place them at the foot of the Cross and be ever so grateful for every blessing. His timing is perfect. His love is perfect. How incredible it is to know that He desires us to find satisfaction in our lives and that you and I were created to fellowship with Him. His timing ... our time. His master plan ... our incredible future.

Love today—live in it and in every single moment life offers you today. Love, like Him, with an abandonment separating the layers of earthly influence and flesh ... and dig deep into the very reason you're here.

"There is a time for everything, and a season for every activity under the heavens:

A time to be born and a time to die,
A time to plant and a time to uproot,
A time to kill and a time to heal,
a time to tear down and a time to build,
a time to weep and a time to laugh,
a time to mourn and a time to dance,
a time to scatter stones and a time to gather them,
a time to embrace and a time to refrain from embracing,
a time to search and a time to give up,
a time to keep and a time to throw away,
a time to tear and a time to mend,
a time to be silent and a time to speak,
a time to love and a time to hate,
a time for war and a time for peace."

Ecclesiastes 3:1–8

*Are you trusting His timing? Jot down a prayer
below. Commit to trusting Him!*

PHOTO CREDIT: BRANNON NAITO

TO THE UTTERMOST

"Therefore he is able to save completely those
who come to God through him, because he
always lives to intercede for them."

Hebrews 7:25

CHARLES SPURGEON delivered his June 8, 1856, Sabbath evening message on "Salvation to the Uttermost," with Hebrews 7:25 as his Scripture base. In his words:

Nature is the spelling-book of man, in which he may learn his Maker's name, he hath studded it with embroidery, with gold, with gems. There are doctrines of truth in the mighty stars, and there are lessons written on the green earth and in the flowers upspringing from the sod. We read the books of God when we see the storm and tempest, for all things speak as God would have them; and if our ears are open, we may hear the voice of God in the rippling of the rill, in the roll of every thunder, in the brightness of every lightning, in the twinkling of every star, in the budding of every flower. God has written the great book of creation, to teach us what he is—how great, how mighty.[3]

We are so unique. God made us that way. As Spurgeon mentions in his talk, the rocks cannot experience salvation, nor the winds, nor the waves, nor the caves. We, however, were created with a little something special that is hollowed out with His name on it. That special hollowed, hallowed place is called our spirit. That spirit, with bended knee and repentant heart, can be saved to the *uttermost*. Completely. Perfectly. Finally. And for all time and eternity. What a promise! What comfort! We should never have a day when we feel we don't belong. We belong, all right! God is our Father. His name is written on our hearts, and we have a place to call home. He has provided salvation for each one of us. He lovingly guides us, like a Master GPS, continually calculating and recalculating, always gently directing us toward a better, more fulfilling future. What a wonderful opportunity we've been given to be everything we can be while we're here.

Help us, God, to find complete fulfillment in You. Help us to find our purpose within Your will. And thank You, so much, for loving us the way You do. Let this life be more about You and less about us as You continually save us to the uttermost.

Write your thoughts below.

....
....
....
....
....
....
....
....
....
....
....
....

PHOTO CREDIT: MARLENA COMPSTON

FOR MY CHILDREN

Love is the seed I'm planting
That unconditional kind
In my little children
In their sweet and precious minds
Filling their hearts with Jesus
And guiding them the way
That they should go ... so they will know
His faithful love for them awaits.
Someday, when grown, if burdens seem
Much larger than their hopes and dreams
I pray that seed of love once placed
Will never question or erase
Their knowledge of their Heavenly Father
And of His love and saving grace.
And when I'm gone, I pray they'll be
Longing for eternity ...
Both strong and wise in their Savior's ways
Knowing there's no other place
Like in the watch of their Shepherd's eyes
Filled with His tender mercy and grace
And love that they can always find ...
Our Father's unconditional kind.

I encourage you to write your own love letter
or poem to someone special in your life.

FOR MY CHILDREN

PHOTO CREDIT: MARCOS PAULO PRADO

NO REGRETS

"Because of the Lord's great love we are not consumed, for his compassions never fail. They are new every morning; great is your faithfulness."

Lamentations 3:22–23

MY MOTHER USED TO SAY, "Today is the first day of the rest of your life." She couldn't have been more right. Every day, there is a beautiful beginning of our day as the sun rises ... and every evening, there is an ending to it. The sun rises; the sun sets. The Word says in Lamentations that His mercies are new every morning. Every single day, we are presented with an opportunity to make the very best of that day.

No matter our age, we can become so involved with our own world and its busyness that we forget to reach out to those we love. It's so easy to pick up the phone and love on someone for a few minutes. A bouquet of flowers, homemade cookies, or a visit could mean the world to someone.

I think of all the lonely people in the world who have no one. It's been on my mind that every single person needs to know that they are special and that their lives matter.

Lord God, help me to live with no regrets. To daily be reminded of how terribly short life is and that today is the first day of the rest of my life. Help me to make it count—to bring glory to You, Father, and to fulfill the calling You have placed on my life. Forgive everything within me that has gotten ahead of You and can tend to turn things upside down. I will always be grateful that You are not the author of confusion. You bring great peace. You can be trusted from the beginning to the end. No regrets, Father, as I close my eyes to sleep tonight.

Do you have regrets? Why not write each one on a piece of paper and then either bury them in the ground or burn them in a fire pit? TODAY, choose to let go of your regrets.

PHOTO CREDIT: MARLENA COMPSTON

AN ODE OF LOVE

In Memory of My Grandparents, W.S. and Iva Brown

Being family means more than we realize ...
It means that we have a common bond between us
That getting along should be everything
That forgiving should be second nature
That peace should be sought at all costs
That hearts should be conquered
That love should grow stronger
As the years granted us go by.
Those precious people that brought us together in this bond
Are now gone, but the same blood that flowed through their veins
Proceeds, even now, through our own.
We are a family, the very by-products of two hearts,
Hearts interwoven in love more than eight decades ago.
Family means so much and it is so easy to forget ...
How special each person is
How precious each moment should be
How short life is and how beautifully each family represents
The two people that began all this.
Grandma and Grandpa Brown, how we love you.

How we miss you ... and still remember
The aroma of Grandma's cooking in the kitchen every morning at
breakfast
Grandpa sitting on the porch in his rocking chair ... his cane clutched
Between his worn, sunbaked hands,
Grandma as she carefully braided and wrapped her hair
Holding bobby-pins between her teeth
The sound of the screen door slamming as grandkids ran in and out
The back porch where we all sat and ate watermelon and smelled the
lilac bushes ...
These memories we can only hold in our hearts
As we hold both of you now ...
How we long to see you again.
How we want to be a family you'd be proud to call your own ...
We are so very proud to be a part of you ...
We lovingly remain your living legacies.

*I encourage you to write your own love letter or poem
to your family. You can start right here ...*

. . . .

. . . .

. . . .

. . . .

. . . .

. . . .

. . . .

PHOTO CREDIT: ANDREW TE

CHRISTMAS MORNING

"Is there any encouragement from belonging to Christ? Any comfort from his love? Any fellowship together in the Spirit? Are your hearts tender and compassionate? Then make me truly happy by agreeing wholeheartedly with each other, loving one another, and working together with one mind and purpose."

Philippians 2:1–2 (NLT)

THE WIND BLOWING OUTSIDE my window woke me up early Christmas morning. *Thank you, Father, for the sacrifice of your precious Son, sent in the form of a baby through a young girl who was willing to sacrifice everything for Your glory. As You always do, Lord God, in an amazing series of magical, supernatural events, You wrapped Jesus in swaddling clothes, knowing all along His eventual steps toward the Cross—the event that would reconcile us, Your beloved children, to You once again.*

I've been pondering about fellowship and relationships. I recently had a house full of people I love and care about. Fourteen beating hearts, happy smiles, loads of laughter—I couldn't have been happier.

But one Christmas Eve was the first time I'd ever spent that holiday *totally* alone. It made me keenly aware of the fact that I *can* be alone; however, nothing is greater than being with those you love. This makes me think about the interesting possibility that God, in His "incredibleness" before time even began, was lonely for fellowship.

You and I both know He doesn't *need* us, but what if ... what if the Author of the universe decided to create us so He could fellowship with us? The Word speaks in Genesis of God walking in the garden to fellowship with Adam and Eve in the cool of the morning. My grandmother used to sing, "And He walks with me, and He talks with me, and He tells me that I am His own." (The words are from the song "In the Garden.")

Just think of our Heavenly Father creating us, intricately molding us in our mother's womb, so He could bring forth His own children to fellowship with. I so understood that on that Christmas morning while sitting on my couch, wrapped in the snuggle blanket that my oldest son gave me.

As I sat near the Christmas lights softly twinkling in all their glory, I felt a keen knowing that what makes this woman truly content is being with those I love. Hearing their laughter, taking in every breath, and every moment, knowing that moment would never come again.

Father, it's so true that You're not in Heaven waiting for us to fail. You are waiting for that moment of glory when we lift our hearts to Heaven, longing for time with You. You just want to be close to us, and as always, You are a wonderful, precious gentleman, never pushing Your will. Waiting, watching ... just longing for moments of soft prayer to float to Heaven. I believe that You capture those beautiful, swirling sounds in Your Almighty arms and wrap them around Yourself. Your Word says You even store our tears—what a beautiful thought!

This morning, I thank You for Jesus. Thank You for the most glorious and thoughtful gift that could ever be given and placed on a tree in the form of a Cross—the gift of Your life laid down for those You love and long to spend all eternity with.

Outside my window on Christmas morning, lovely blankets and soft drifts of white snow wiped the slate of my entire world pure and beautiful for a new year to begin.

It's truly all about You, Jesus.

Write about a time when you were with those you loved. Then think of a time of solitude when it was just you and the Lord. Describe the emotions or feelings around those two times.

....
....
....
....
....
....
....
....
....
....
....
....
....
....
....
....

PHOTO CREDIT: TIRAYA ADAM

SAMSON AND DELILAH

*"And we all, who with unveiled faces contemplate
the Lord's glory, are being transformed into
his image with ever-increasing glory, which
comes from the Lord, who is the Spirit."*

2 Corinthians 3:18

SAMSON'S CALLING WAS MADE KNOWN to his parents even before he was born. He was the fulfillment of a promise to his parents, and they took great measures to follow God's instructions to rear him correctly. When he was young, he was loyal to God. As Samson grew up, he began to have an appetite for things outside of God's design for him. Does that sound familiar to anyone?

Once grown, he manipulated his parents so he could marry a woman he shouldn't have married. It was a marriage that had nothing but heartbreak for him. Then, out of anger and great disappointment, he fell in love with Delilah and ushered into his life a very deceptive, scheming, and dark force. His lust for Delilah and his determination to win her love proved nothing but emptiness for him. Sadly, Samson compromised the beautiful gift that had been given to him before birth—the tremendous calling to free God's people. His disobedience and irresponsibility cost him so much.

When we look at Delilah and her motives, we see that she had a selfish agenda. She wanted to bring Samson down, all the while lining her pockets with silver willingly paid to her by the Philistines. Samson's agenda was ultimately love and happiness, but both escaped him. Delilah, it appears, was sent into his life to destroy his confidence, steal his joy, thwart the call on his life, and set him up for complete failure. She clung to him like a bad grape on a green vine. As powerful as Samson was and as anointed as his life had been, he just could never prune Delilah from his life.

We must remember that Samson was as human as we are. *If only* he had focused on the call on his life. *If only* he had bent his knee and his heart totally to God and waited on God's timing. Instead, he was continually sought after by his Philistine enemies. He was betrayed by the woman he desired to share his life with, he chose to compromise the calling on his life, and, devastatingly, he lost his life.

In looking over the entire story of Samson, I see the following truths:

In his anger and disappointment, **Samson's faith decreased**.

In his desire to fulfill his life outside of God, **Samson lost his focus**.

As he continued in his disobedience, **Samson's power was compromised**.

Ultimately, **Samson's life was extinguished**.

May we never allow *anything* or *anyone* to pull us down into an abyss that causes us to lose ourselves. May we never lose our focus. May we never be willing to give up our dreams or our calling and purpose. May we choose to be *overcomers* and *never* be overcome … except by our Savior, who *always* causes us to be powerful and confident in Him.

I choose to follow Him and fulfill the call on my life. My favorite Scripture, Psalm 37:4, says, "Take delight in the Lord, and he will give you the desires of your heart." May our hearts be divinely focused. May our desire be to love Him. May our lives not even have a *hint* of disobedience but of confidence in who we are in Him.

How does this devotion speak to your heart? Do you have times when you say, "If only ..."? God can redeem ALL your regrets.

PHOTO CREDIT: KARSTEN WINEGEART

MORE THAN A CONQUEROR

"For in the day of trouble he will keep me safe in his dwelling; he will hide me in the shelter of his sacred tent and set me high upon a rock."

Psalm 27:5

IN HIS BOOK *My Utmost for His Highest*, Oswald Chambers wrote: "Our yesterdays present irreparable things to us; it is true that we have lost opportunities which will never return, but God can transform this destructive anxiety into a constructive thoughtfulness for the future. Let the past sleep, but let it sleep on the bosom of Christ. Leave the Irreparable Past in His hands and step out into the Irresistible Future with Him."[4]

Oswald Chambers also said, "Prayer does not equip us for greater works—prayer is the greater work."[5]

Father God, You are the lover of my soul, my gatekeeper, the One who sees what my life is all about. I praise You for making me more than a conqueror, an overcomer, a visionary, a listener of Your voice, a seeker of Your will—You, Father, are truly awesome! Help me, dear Lord, to raise my head up and walk boldly through this life ... full of grace, unwavering, and with a spirit of love, even when it's the most difficult. Father, I ask for simplicity, consistency, commitment, assurance, holiness, trust, restoration, authority, submission, and clarity. You never leave us; You never forsake us. I am so very grateful for who You are and for the promise of a great and wonderful future. Amen.

Write your own prayer here.

....
....
....
....
....
....
....
....
....
....
....
....
....
....
....
....
....
....
....
....

PHOTO CREDIT: NELLIA KURME

DISTRACTIONS

*"We demolish arguments and every pretension that
sets itself up against the knowledge of God, and we take
captive every thought to make it obedient to Christ."*

2 Corinthians 10:5

THE LORD IS SO FAITHFUL. As I was lying on the couch, wrapped up in a blanket and not feeling well *at all*, my thoughts were on how distracting the world can be. Think of how *many* thoughts go through our heads in just one day!

The Word says to "take every thought captive" (2 Corinthians 10:5). Just think of what we might go through in one morning: The alarm goes off, we're out of bed, and immediately, thoughts begin "streaming" through our minds.

The Word speaks of Jesus starting His day in the early morning. Mark 1:35 says, "Very early in the morning, while it was still dark, Jesus got up, left the house and went off to a solitary place, where he prayed." The Lord knew He needed a "game plan" for the day, and He wanted to spend time with His Father.

I must admit that I am *so* much more a "night person" than a "morning person." I get drops into my spirit more in the late-night hours (or while I'm driving). This is just what works for me, but what a better plan it could be to get up early and seek Him first—before the day truly begins! Maybe then, all the crazy thoughts that drift through our minds could be spiritually filtered *first* before they start.

I hope the traffic's not bad … What to wear … Is it cold outside? … What about that meeting today? … Oh my, I wish I hadn't said that yesterday … What if I lost my health, job, spouse, friends, etc.? What if … what if … what if …

See where our heads can take us? Let's make a simple choice to seek Him early, seek His design and desire for the day, and then place all our cares and concerns at the foot of the Cross and just walk away.

Distractions don't have to rule us. Distractions don't have to define us. Father God, help us to take "every single thought captive." What does that really mean? It means to discipline your mind so it's not on a merry-go-round that never stops. *You* determine what comes through your thoughts. You don't entertain every random thought that hits your mind. Take hold of a foundation within your thoughts and stand firmly in what you truly *know*.

"Finally, brethren, whatever things are true, whatever things are noble, whatever things are just, whatever things are pure, whatever things are lovely, whatever things are of good report, if there is any virtue and if there is anything praiseworthy—meditate on these things. The things which you learned and received and heard and saw in me, these do, and the God of peace will be with you" (Philippians 4:8–9, NKJV).

What are your distractions? When do you spend your quiet time with Him? Seek first His kingdom … and all these things will be added to you: peace, joy, provision, hope, and more!

PHOTO CREDIT: EDI LIBEDINKSY

MAKE A DIFFERENCE

*"Do not conform to the pattern of this world, but
be transformed by the renewing of your mind. Then
you will be able to test and approve what God's
will is—his good, pleasing and perfect will."*

Romans 12:2

SIMPLE QUESTION: Are we all broken? Pretty much. As we begin
to heal, and continue to heal, let us choose to make a difference in this life. So,
basically, we can "look out for number one" by acknowledging who *is* "number
one." And ... come to terms with the fact that it's *not* us!

The Word says to be salt and light. To choose life. To cling to Him. To not
conform to this world but to be transformed. How? By renewing our mind,
being in the Word, and allowing the Holy Spirit to mold us and grow us. He
certainly will be faithful to do exactly that. Side note: In His time, not ours.

I promise ... it is so rewarding to share the Lord Jesus Christ and explain
to someone their very own personalized gift of salvation. Especially when
they feel hopeless, and you stand in awe, watching Him navigate futures and
transform lives. I promise He is a faithful character builder and a confidence
instiller, and He has the nurturing heart of a mother, yet He is most certainly
a compassionate and caring Father.

Where do you need to stop conforming to this world? What do you need to lay down so you can choose to be salt and light instead?

PHOTO CREDIT: PAIGE CODY

BEAUTIFUL PAGES

"The heart of the discerning acquires knowledge,
for the ears of the wise seek it out."

Proverbs 18:15

BOOKS. *I love books*. I mean, I *REALLY* love books. I have books ranging from J. Oswald Sanders' *Spiritual Leadership* to a collection of *Southern Living* cookbooks. Yes, I read cookbooks, too.

I have my favorite books, such as *The Confident Woman* by Ingrid Trobisch. Ingrid was a beautiful-spirited former missionary who was married to missionary Walter Trobisch. The name of Ingrid's home was *Haus Geborgenheit*, which is German for "a place of steadfast shelter." Isn't that beautiful? She tells the story of one of her mother's last Christmas letters that stated: "My hands tremble, my legs are unsteady, but my heart is strong and my love for you is unchanging." THAT statement alone could change many a heart that feels alone in the world.

The great thing about a wonderful book is that we can *feel* it in our hands. Not only can we feel the bound book in our hands, but we can take a pen and write all over it like it's a prayer journal if we want to—and believe me, *I do*! We can underline precious words of wisdom. We can date our journal entries and then, years later, take the book from the shelf, dust it off, and treasure it just like we would a faithful friend. It's like it's brand-new again as we read the words we wrote in years gone by—filling our heart, once again, with the book's knowledge.

I just pulled out a few of my favorite books tonight and read through some of the entries I'd like to share with you. I'm happy to open my journals to you because it's part of the call on my life. To expose my heart might help point you to His heart. To be real with you might hit something in you that will cause you to launch and reach for your *full* potential!

Here's a journal entry I dated October 23, 1999, in a book by the anointed Beth Moore called *A Heart Like His*:

"Heavenly Father, As I begin this journey this night, I simply must lift my heart, my hands and the Spirit within me to You! YOU ARE WORTHY OF PRAISE! You are Holy, O Lord Most High! Thank You for being the jealous God You are! For pursuing me without ever abandoning me—for loving me without ever pushing me away—for seeing through all my insecurities, inabilities, and the girl's heart within me. For I truly know that You love me with an everlasting love!"[6]

Those words are so meaningful to me, and they give me such a glimpse as to exactly where I was late one night in 1999. In the first Bible my parents gave me on December 25, 1971, I wrote the words of my former pastor, Andrew O'Kelley: "Expect Jesus any minute, but live like it will be one hundred years!"

While teaching a women's Bible study, I penned a quote found in the book *Captivating* by John and Stasi Eldredge: "Your heart as a woman is the most important thing about you." Just beautiful.

Last, I'll share what I wrote in my copy of *Executive EQ* while in Chicago one winter. It was 11 p.m. on Friday, December 3, and snow was gently falling outside. I was alone in the restaurant on the first floor of the Drake Hotel. A piano was being played softly in the background, and there was low hustle and bustle all around me. I was in my own "reading world." I can still remember the smell in the air as I took my pen and wrote, "What an amazing journey 2010 has been! 2011 will prove to be even more exciting and [there are] so many dynamics of life to discover! I can't WAIT to see what all God has in store!"

In closing, books have the most beautiful pages between their front and back covers, and, most importantly for me, part of my life is lovingly tucked between the pages with my written prayers and journaling.

Are you also a reader? Do you journal in your books? What is your favorite book or author?

....
....
....
....
....
....
....
....
....
....
....
....
....
....
....
....
....
....

PHOTO CREDIT: DEBBE 'SUNNY' BROAM

SURRENDER

"'Love the Lord your God with all your heart and with all your soul and with all your strength and with all your mind'; and 'Love your neighbor as yourself.'"

Luke 10:27

WE SAY, "God, you can have everything in my life, but *please* ... not that one small area ... that one small chamber in my heart. No. Not that." But He is *faithful* to want the diamond that is buried in the darkest chambers of your heart. He isn't nearly as interested in the small stones that are easy for you to give up, those that are superficially lying in the first couple layers within your heart. He wants the perfect diamond that must be carefully and patiently excavated, for *this* is what holds the key to your deepest fears and your *greatest freedom*. He wants the key to unlock those doors and unleash joy and strength in your heart.

Remember that He is a gentleman and will never force His way. He is waiting for you to ask Him in. Let me encourage you to surrender that which is buried. Allow Him to resurrect the death inside your heart to release an amazing *gust* of new life from within you.

Breathe IN forgiveness ... EXHALE bitterness.

Breathe IN laughter ... EXHALE sorrow.

Breathe IN lightheartedness ... EXHALE heaviness.

Embrace a new beginning and *let go* of the old, dead, rotting bones, knowing *fully* that *He* is the power, the resurrection, and the life—the *Life Giver*.

Choose *this* day, the Word states, whom you will serve. Are you just dead, dry bones with hidden, buried diamonds—or a *powerful* man or woman of God who can *stretch your arms* before Heaven and say, "Oh God, use me for Your purposes ... for YOUR glory. You can have access to every place, Lord. Every chamber is yours."

This is the cry of my heart for you. This is the prayer within me for your complete and total healing. *You* are why I wrote this book.

Surrender to Him. It will be THE BEST DECISION you have ever made in your life.

....
....
....
....
....
....
....
....
....
....
....
....
....

PHOTO CREDIT: BEN WHITE

BROUGHT TO MY KNEES

"Oh come, let us worship and bow down; Let us kneel
before the Lord our Maker. For He is our God, and we are
the people of His pasture, And the sheep of His hand."

Psalm 95:6–7 (NKJV)

I RECENTLY HEARD A SONG called "Brought to My Knees." You know me—as I drove home, I started pondering the significance of kneeling in prayer. I searched and found several thoughts about this. Kneeling seems to be the most beautiful expression of surrendering as we pray. To kneel is to show a submission of our focus and thoughts during our time of fellowship with our Savior.

In Acts 7:59–60 (NKJV), we read, "And they stoned Stephen as he was calling on God and saying, 'Lord Jesus, receive my spirit.' Then he knelt down and cried out with a loud voice, 'Lord, do not charge them with this sin.'" That brings tears to my eyes. Stephen, in the last moments of his life, certainly in distress and much pain, fell to his knees before God in total submission. He was completely innocent of any charges, yet just as our Lord Jesus did on the Cross, he cried out for God not to hold that charge against the very ones who were taking his life.

In the Gospel of Mark, we read how Jesus was in a stressful time right before He was given over to be crucified. Feeling very troubled, deeply distressed, and sorrowful, he fell on the ground in prayer to pour His heart out before His Heavenly Father.

"And He took Peter, James, and John with Him, and He began to be troubled and deeply distressed. Then He said to them, 'My soul is exceedingly sorrowful, even to death. Stay here and watch.' He went a little farther, and fell on the ground, and prayed that if it were possible, the hour might pass from Him. And He said, 'Abba, Father, all things are possible for You. Take this cup away from Me; nevertheless, not what I will, but what You will'" (Mark 14:33–36, NKJV).

You can hear the humility in His prayer—the choice He made to be completely emptied of Himself as He was on His knees, crying out to God for help through these very dark moments of anxiety.

In my Scripture search, I also found a journal entry I wrote on December 10, 1997, in my *Max Lucado Inspirational Study Bible*:

My Bible sits there faithfully
Full of wisdom, full of prayers
All the answers that I need
With head bowed and bended knee.
Lord, help me to seek You every day
Help me to love in every way
To mirror Your life, Your special grace
Help me always seek your face.

I leave you with the thought of finding a quiet place today and bending your knee to Him in worship and adoration. Pour out your heart before Him and listen as He pours out His heart to you.

PHOTO CREDIT: JOHN MOESES BAUAN

HOMELESS HEART

"For I know the plans I have for you," declares
the Lord, "plans to prosper you and not to harm
you, plans to give you hope and a future."

Jeremiah 29:11

AS I WAS DRIVING EAST on a highway, I passed a man who appeared homeless, picking up cans on the side of the road. My heart went out to him, and I lifted him up in prayer, asking the Lord about him. At sixty-five miles per hour, I only saw him briefly. What I did catch was his tattered clothing, weathered profile, and a stocking cap on top of his long, scraggly silver hair. *Please, Lord, bless him*, I prayed.

Miles down the road, I was still thinking about what happened in his life for him to be where he was. Maybe he lost his family? His home? His ability to support himself?

The message that came to me was wondering where YOU are today. Do you need a home for your heart? Have you found yourself feeling bankrupt in life and wondering if things will ever get better? Did you lose your way somewhere along the road of life? Take a wrong turn or lose your direction? Maybe someone left you on the side of the road, alone and sitting with an empty tank. Are you picking up trash along the side of the highways named depression, discouragement, or unforgiveness?

According to Ephesians, we have been given a *glorious inheritance*! God never created you with any intention of dropping you on the side of a desolate highway ... all alone and without purpose. He has promises all throughout the Word that you can get into your head and your heart to better understand what your life is about.

One of my favorite Scriptures is Jeremiah 29:11—"'For I know the plans I have for you,' declares the Lord, 'plans to prosper you and not to harm you, plans to give you hope and a future.'" There have been times in my life when I held on to that verse like it was my *very breath*. I encourage you to read it every single day until that knowledge moves from your head to your heart and from your heart to your head. Write it down and place it in front of you. Determine that your heart will *no longer* remain without a home. Take yourself off the side of the highway today.

Get back on the road to finding your place in this world. Get in the Word, which is your map, and you will find the directions to everything you need. It will be so worth the journey!

Does your heart have a home? Declare today to place your faith in Him every single day.

PHOTO CREDIT: PAUL SKORUPSKAS

FOCUS, THEN TRUST

*"Wait for the Lord; be strong and take
heart and wait for the Lord."*

Psalm 27:14

QUESTION POSED: Where is your focus? It's so easy to focus on other things besides what we should be focusing on ... or should I say, *who* we should be focusing on. I, for one, am guilty.

I recently talked with a dear friend who had ended a relationship. Immediately, my friend's thoughts were to get on a dating website and start looking for love again. My advice to my friend was: 1) give yourself time to heal; 2) don't buy into the world's way of finding the right one; and most importantly, 3) *please* allow God time to bring the right person into your life. Disclaimer: I *do* know several couples who met through a dating site, so don't think it "can't ever happen." Just be cautious, as there are many lost souls merely looking for a place to land.

Here's the truth: God's plan is perfect. His timing is perfect. My concern for my friend is that they will go right back into the cycle of dating, get caught up in the whole thing again, and then be right back in a "wrong" relationship again, thus wasting precious time.

God wants us to *focus* on Him—and even better, to *trust* Him completely! That's something I have had to deal with. *Have I trusted Him?* I trust Him with my salvation (that He so lovingly imparts), and I trust Him with the care of my children (that He so graciously shares), but I was not trusting Him with other important issues in my life.

There's *so* much more to life than choosing to go down the wrong path. It's simple to make those paths straight. Start by *trusting* Him. *Trust* Him. *Trust* Him! What truly do you have to *lose*?

Did you know that one definition of *trust* is "assured reliance on the character, ability, strength, or truth of someone or something"? God wants to help us from our head to our heart—and then from our heart to our head. Read the definition of trust again with the focus on trusting God: *assured reliance on the character, ability, and strength* of a Heavenly Father who has such a glorious, great promise of a future for each one of us! You see, *His* plan for us is so much more creative and colorful and exciting than we could possibly dream up ourselves! And, best of all, He sees us through the blood of Jesus ... completely redeemed.

Yes, it's true, we mess up, but *that's* what it's all about. He continues to stretch out His arms to us like the faithful Heavenly Father He is ... never letting go. He always focuses on us, believes in us, and is on our side.

Write the definition of trust below. Know that He has a great plan for you. Begin trusting Him with all the details of your life.

....

....

....

....

....

PHOTO CREDIT: MELISSA ASKEW

JUST AS I AM

"In all these things we are more than conquerors through Him who loved us. For I am persuaded that neither death nor life, nor angels nor principalities nor powers, nor things present nor things to come, nor height nor depth, nor any other created thing, shall be able to separate us from the love of God which is in Christ Jesus our Lord."

Romans 8:37–39, NKJV

EXPECTATIONS. Offenses. Criticisms. Judgments. We can place so much weight on others … and even on ourselves. Remember that old hymn "Just as I Am"? It was written in 1836 by a woman named Charlotte Elliott. It's an interesting story. A man she met had presented the gospel to her, and she was quite offended by the way he presented it to her. Weeks later, she confessed she was earnestly seeking her Savior and asked the same man who had previously offended her to lead the way for her to know her Savior.

I've taken the liberty of placing a more modern twist to two of the stanzas in her famous hymn:

Just as I am, though tossed about
With many a conflict, many a doubt
Fightings and fears within, without

O Lamb of God, I come, I come.

Just as I am, poor, wretched, blind;

Sight, riches, healing of the mind,

Yes, all I need is You to find

O Lamb of God, I come, I come.

Are there criticisms all around you because you don't fit someone else's mold of who you are supposed to be? Expectations laid out by others about what you're supposed to look like? Act like? Dress like? *Know this!* You are precious just as you are. His Word says that He's changing us from "glory to glory." Every day, we live and breathe and learn and see. Yes, we may fall but only to wake up the next morning with a clean slate and a new day!

If anyone has spoken against you, or if you have placed far too much pressure on your own shoulders, then *lay it down* and stretch your arms to the Heavens. Breathe IN ... breathe OUT ... and say, "I am loved *just as I am*." It's truly that simple. Get it from your head to your heart ... and then from your heart to your head.

Say out loud, "I am loved JUST AS I AM." Jesus loves you with every drop of blood He shed on the Cross. AND ... He would have done the same thing if it were ONLY YOU.

....

....

....

....

....

....

PHOTO CREDIT: AIONY HAUST

BROKEN HEARTS
CAN BE MENDED

*"Jesus said, 'Father, forgive them, for they
do not know what they are doing.'"*

Luke 23:34

A FRIEND TOLD ME that due to her husband cheating on her, she thought she could never trust again. I have meditated on her comments and prayed over them to receive some revelation about these feelings of devastation and hurt. A few insights came to my heart, and I want to share them with you. I've written this to give you hope if you have found yourself in this situation.

First, I believe the person who cheated didn't do it to hurt you. People who cheat do this because there is (or was) a huge hole in their heart that only God can fill. They are unhappy and always seeking something or someone to make them happy. You could have done everything in life perfectly with a capital "P" and still found yourself in a relationship with this person. They have huge, gaping wounds that need to be healed. The *only One* who can heal them is Jesus.

Let's visit the Garden of Eden, where Adam and Eve lived in a pure and perfect world. Even though life was great, they still chose to break God's trust and covenant. They decided to "cheat" on God, believing the grass was greener on the other side. Their decision hurt the heart of God deeply. It certainly did not catch Him by surprise, but their choice severed the wonderful relationship they had enjoyed with God. The closeness was gone. The deep intimacy and walks in the Garden were history. As we all know, there were far-reaching consequences for their actions that we still suffer today. *But ...* God had a plan!

The garments the Lord God made for Adam and Eve didn't come free; a spotless lamb was sacrificed to cover their sin. Much later, another Lamb was sacrificed. As the Lamb of God hung on the Cross, many stood below him, hurling insults and directing their anger and bitterness toward Him.

Notice this, though! He didn't rebuke them! He didn't respond to their painful insults, hurled fists, and cutting words. He turned His bleeding head toward Heaven and prayed to the Father *for* them. "Jesus said, "Father, forgive them, for they do not know what they are doing" (Luke 23:34). What an amazing statement of love and humility! Jesus's ego was not in the way. He wasn't demanding His rights. He simply prayed for those who so deeply hurt Him. They didn't take His life—He willingly laid it down for all of us.

The truth is this: People hurt us. Some mean to; some do not. Some just truly don't know any better because they are so wounded themselves. God never intended for you to go through the hurts you have endured. The *good news* is that we can have *Kingdom living* right here within our own hearts. God is our Protector and Shield. Through giving His ALL for us, Jesus chose forgiveness and understood that those who hurt Him didn't truly understand the fullness of their actions.

Should we forgive? Yes. Do we forget? That will be between you, the circumstance, and our Heavenly Father. The best part is that your past hurts don't equal your future. There is a beautiful, golden plan for you. Step into it today and humble yourself before God. I encourage you to write down the names of those who have hurt you, cheated on you, or deserted you. Ask God to help you forgive every single name. Then, tear up that piece of paper and toss it in the trash or burn it in a fire pit. Choose freedom from any scars that were placed on your heart! Today is your day of freedom!

This is the beginning of your list. Use separate pages if you need to. It's time to forgive those who have hurt you, cheated on you, lied about you, and devastated you. Simply write their names. God knows the situations. TODAY is a great day to place it under the blood and begin to forgive. The Holy Spirit gives us the power to do exactly that: FORGIVE.

PHOTO CREDIT: AARON BURDEN

AMAZING WORDS

"You, my brothers and sisters, were called to be free. But do not use your freedom to indulge the flesh; rather, serve one another humbly in love. For the entire law is fulfilled in keeping this one command: "Love your neighbor as yourself." If you bite and devour each other, watch out or you will be destroyed by each other. So I say, walk by the Spirit, and you will not gratify the desires of the flesh. For the flesh desires what is contrary to the Spirit, and the Spirit what is contrary to the flesh. They are in conflict with each other, so that you are not to do whatever you want. But if you are led by the Spirit, you are not under the law. The acts of the flesh are obvious: sexual immorality, impurity and debauchery; idolatry and witchcraft; hatred, discord, jealousy, fits of rage, selfish ambition, dissensions, factions and envy; drunkenness, orgies, and the like. I warn you, as I did before, that those who live like this will not inherit the kingdom of God. But the fruit of the Spirit is love, joy, peace, forbearance, kindness, goodness, faithfulness, gentleness and self-control. Against such things there is no law. Those who belong to Christ Jesus have crucified the flesh with its passions and desires. Since we live by

*the Spirit, let us keep in step with the Spirit. Let us not
become conceited, provoking and envying each other."*

Galatians 5:13–26

So much wisdom and truth in this passage! Wrap your head and heart around each one. Meditate on them. Allow the Holy Spirit to teach you. If you have not taken that step quite yet, *today* can be *your* day of salvation.

***Is your heart where it needs to be? Where are you struggling
today? Pray for peace. Ask God to continue healing
you through and through. Be prepared—He will!***

....

....

....

....

....

....

....

....

....

....

....

....

PHOTO CREDIT: VALIANT MADE

KNOW YOUR TRIBE

"I alone cannot change the world, but I can cast a stone across the waters to create many ripples."

Mother Teresa

REMEMBER THAT AS WE STEP INTO each new day, not everyone will be on our same page. Not everyone will believe in what we do or want to be a part of it. But remember, there are those who will embrace us. *They* will welcome the gifts, talents, and skills we bring. *They* will need what we have. *They* are the ones we are called to. *They* are our tribe.

Do you know who your support system is?

....

....

....

....

....

PHOTO CREDIT: DEBBIE 'SUNNY' BROAM

GOD KNOWS

"For we do not have a High Priest who cannot sympathize with our weaknesses, but was in all points tempted as we are, yet without sin."

Hebrews 4:15 (NKJV)

ANGER CAN CERTAINLY disguise itself. Many people are just bottom-line angry with God. We can get stuck in the grieving process: denial, anger, bitterness, and grief. Maybe our circumstances aren't what we had hoped, or maybe we've experienced loss. We might be feeling forgotten, broken, left out, or abandoned.

God knows. Share it with Him. I encourage you to pray. Ask the Lord to reveal any anger that is stored within you. Then, begin sifting through it, all the while praying, until nothing is left but ashes that can be blown away with one strong breath.

Share your thoughts after reading this. Pray and expose the anger within. It is SO worth it. Begin dealing with it this very day.

PHOTO CREDIT: WESLEY TINGEY

HIS SPOKEN WORDS

"I will give you a new heart and put a new spirit within you; I will take the heart of stone out of your flesh and give you a heart of flesh. I will put My Spirit within you and cause you to walk in My statutes, and you will keep My judgments and do them."

Ezekiel 36:26–27 (NKJV)

DRIVING TO WORK ONE DAY, I thought about how faithful God is. He is true to His Word. I remembered many words He's spoken personally to my heart over the last ten years ...

"It is well with my soul." This was His message to me during a troubled time—words to remind me that HE is in control and guiding my journey. It's *my* lesson to learn to trust Him. It's easy to trust Him with our salvation; that seems a given. It's not difficult for me to trust Him with my children and their lives; however, there are one or two areas in my life where I realize I don't give Him full access. His words, simply put: "Marlena, let it be well with your soul and trust Me!"

Or these words: "I am under no obligation to bless you when you choose to step into something I didn't first begin." It's a hard lesson when we follow a path that God is saying no to.

371

"I am longsuffering, but I have a limit." Only a loving Father would speak these words. When we're off too far to the right or the left, He will lovingly guide us back to center. That's a promise!

"Don't fight, for I will take care of you." And after nine years of being on my own again, He has proven Himself faithful to these words spoken to me in 2001.

"If I have to make you a fool to make you wise, I will do so." That was a tough lesson many years ago that taught me to discern those who care about me and those who don't. No matter the situation or relationship, realize that everyone won't be your best friend. Learn to lean on God and not on people. He's our acceptance, and He's more than enough.

"Let go." Hard words to receive when you don't want to hear those words. Have you ever asked God for an answer to a prayer, and when He finally answered, the answer was far different than what you had planned or hoped for? He *knows* what is best! He knows the plans He has for you—therefore, best to listen and "let go."

I'm learning more and more to be obedient to His Word and to the words He speaks to me personally. Have you ever heard this phrase: "Slow obedience is no obedience"? Let us be "immediately" obedient once He pierces our heart with truth. Our best is at the center of our Father's heart. We can trust that and never doubt it. We are dearly loved and given the gift of eternity.

What is God speaking to your heart today?

....

....

....

PHOTO CREDIT: JONATHAN KEMPER

THE FULL ARMOR OF GOD

*"Finally, be strong in the Lord and in his mighty power.
Put on the full armor of God, so that you can take your
stand against the devil's schemes. For our struggle is not
against flesh and blood, but against the rulers, against
the authorities, against the powers of this dark world
and against the spiritual forces of evil in the heavenly
realms. Therefore put on the full armor of God, so that
when the day of evil comes, you may be able to stand your
ground, and after you have done everything, to stand.
Stand firm then, with the belt of truth buckled around
your waist, with the breastplate of righteousness in place,
and with your feet fitted with the readiness that comes
from the gospel of peace. In addition to all this, take up
the shield of faith, with which you can extinguish all
the flaming arrows of the evil one. Take the helmet of
salvation and the sword of the Spirit, which is the word
of God. And pray in the Spirit on all occasions with all
kinds of prayers and requests. With this in mind, be alert
and always keep on praying for all the Lord's people."*

Ephesians 6:10–18

Put on your armor every day. Be well-equipped and prepared.

PHOTO CREDIT: BAS VAN DEN EIJKHOF

CLARITY OF A DIAMOND

*"I delight greatly in the Lord; my soul rejoices in my
God. For he has clothed me with garments of salvation
and arrayed me in a robe of his righteousness, as
a bridegroom adorns his head like a priest, and
as a bride adorns herself with her jewels."*

Isaiah 61:10

THE DIAMOND IS THE MOST precious of all stones. It is
white in color and beautifully transparent. I've learned that diamond clarity
describes either the absence or presence of flaws inside or on the surface of the
diamond. A perfect stone with perfect clarity or clearness is rare, and most
flaws that do exist can't be seen without looking at them through a jeweler's
magnifying glass.

*Oh, Lord, may our hearts be beautifully transparent before You! May our
hearts be lovingly transparent toward those around us. May we be REAL and not
a false version of ourselves, but what You desire for us to be—genuine.*

The verses in Isaiah speak of our soul rejoicing in Him, and isn't it amazing
that He clothes us with garments of salvation and then arrays us in a robe of
His righteousness? Notice that these are things *He* takes care of—we must
have a willing heart and one that delights and rejoices in Him.

Lord, help us to have the clarity of a flawless diamond. Though knowing we will never be completely perfect while in this world, we can certainly trust You to polish and refine us as You move us toward the plan You have purposed for our lives.

Let the paragraph above be your prayer. Write it out or make it your own by writing it in your own words.

PHOTO CREDIT: MARLENA COMPSTON

A GLIMPSE OF PARADISE AND POVERTY

"I pray that God, the source of hope, will fill you completely with joy and peace because you trust in him. Then you will overflow with confident hope through the power of the Holy Spirit."

Romans 15:13 (NLT)

ARRIVING IN COZUMEL, I loaded my bags into the tiny rental car, a Dodge Attitude, and took off, windows down. The streets were filled with happy, Spanish-speaking voices, and festive music blared from the radio. I zipped around the streets like I owned the place! It didn't take me long to figure out that I was going the wrong way on a one-way street. This is something even a language barrier will help you figure out when the locals are laughing and flailing their arms and pointing to a one-way street sign above their heads!

After I turned myself around and quit giggling, I found myself in a neighborhood not far from the airport. One thing I learned is that the locals are only allowed to use their water during certain parts of the day. Everywhere I looked, bright-colored laundry was hung out to dry in the warm sunshine.

No doubt, poverty was living among these residents like a dirty, unwelcome rat. Within moments, I found the main road near the ocean where tourism and shopping began. There were literally fifteen to twenty jewelry stores filled with gold and silver along a quarter-mile stretch of beachfront property. Much activity filled the street as huge cruise ships unloaded hundreds of people anxious to find a bargain in Cozumel. Just a few miles down the road were some of the beautiful, all-inclusive resorts—with, of course, an unlimited water supply and huge swimming pools.

What struck me that first day was the fact that, as I drove through the poverty-hit areas a few blocks away from downtown, I found nothing but smiling, happy people. Children on old bicycles were laughing and playing, and clunky old scooters were zipping here and there carrying two to three people on one scooter. The people were just happy, all the while basking in this beautiful city! It certainly seemed to me that they didn't know they were doing without. Maybe they had made peace with it all and chose to shield themselves from the glitz and glamour of their city, knowing that's just not reality for them.

Everyone I met looked at me kindly with big brown eyes, willing to help me even if I was lost, couldn't speak their language, and didn't know which direction to go! It amazes me still that in Cozumel, paradise and poverty live so closely within reach of each other, and life just ... well ... goes on.

How true that often seems of our lives! We are able, and we have the God-given right, to be living in the neighborhood of "paradise," but we choose to live on the streets of poverty within our minds and hearts. We choose to live on Victim Street with no roadmap to escape.

Deuteronomy 30:15–16 says, "See, I set before you today life and prosperity, death and destruction. For I command you today to love the Lord your God, to walk in obedience to him, and to keep his commands, decrees and laws; then you will live and increase, and the Lord your God will bless you in the land you are entering to possess."

We are given this promise and have the right to choose life—and a *good* life! How many times I personally have chosen the wrong path, ignored the road signs pointing the right way, and continued into a place I should never have been in the first place! If you are in the midst of a wrong direction in your life—and you *know* you are headed down the wrong path—*stop* and redirect your heart toward prosperity in your life and away from death and destruction.

I am flailing my arms at you to get your attention! The Lord's promises are *many*! They are everlasting and are stamped with a promise of His love and care for you. You absolutely matter! Today, get a glimpse of your life in a state of "paradise" that includes joy, health, love, peace, contentment, provision for more than enough, and a *fantastic future* beyond your wildest imagination!

This is all within your reach, but *you must choose it*! Today, leave the streets of poverty, including spiritual bankruptcy, stress, depression, discouragement, greed, or rebellion, far behind you. Now you can walk into a much brighter future and a life of paradise all your own.

Have riches owned you? Choose today to repent and ask
God to place you on the right path of honoring Him in
everything you do. Riches will NEVER satisfy you.

PHOTO CREDIT: ALFONSO SCARPA

ARMS OF
LOVE

"Be strong in the Lord and in his mighty power."

Ephesians 6:10

WE CAN FIND GREAT PEACE knowing that God is our refuge.
He is our Rock, the One who arms us with strength!

"As for God, his way is perfect:
The Lord's word is flawless;
he shields all who take refuge in him.
For who is God besides the Lord?
And who is the Rock except our God?
It is God who arms me with strength
and keeps my way secure.
He makes my feet like the feet of a deer;
he causes me to stand on the heights.
He trains my hands for battle;
my arms can bend a bow of bronze.
You make your saving help my shield,
and your right hand sustains me;

your help has made me great.
You provide a broad path for my feet,
so that my ankles do not give way."

Psalm 18:30–36

Father, remind us that You are there, ready to hold us up even when we feel we cannot possibly stand on our own strength. You want us to be strong in You and in the power of Your might. We may not be able, but You are WELL able. We may not feel strong, but You, Lord God, are STRONG.

We are at the end of Love Illuminated. *How has this book helped your spiritual life? List moments that have drawn you closer to Him.*

....

....

....

....

....

....

....

....

....

....

ENDNOTES

1   William J. Johnson, *George Washington, The Christian*, published in 1919.

2   "What Does It Mean to Be Pure in Heart?" gotquestions.org, https://www.gotquestions.org/pure-in-heart.html.

3   Charles Spurgeon, "Salvation to the Uttermost," June 8, 1856, The Spurgeon Center for Preaching at Midwestern Seminary, https://www.spurgeon.org/resource-library/sermons/salvation-to-the-uttermost/#flipbook/.

4   Oswald Chambers, "Yesterday," *My Utmost for His Highest*, utmost.org, December 31, https://utmost.org/modern-classic/yesterday/.

5   Chambers, *My Utmost for His Highest*, October 17.

6   Beth Moore, *A Heart Like His: Intimate Reflections on the Life of David* (B&H Publishing Group, 1999).

LETTER TO THE READER

In *Love Illuminated: A Devotional Journal to Awaken and Deepen Your Faith*, I ask you, as a reader, to review and share your experience through this journey. As others read your experience, they will gain interest and hope to bring about a change in their own lives. As an independent author, reviews play a crucial role in helping me reach a broader audience and allow me to continue creating content that resonates with readers like you. If you have a moment, I would be incredibly grateful if you could share your thoughts on *Love Illuminated* by leaving reviews on bookseller sites and other platforms where you purchased or discovered my book. Sharing on your own social media platforms greatly helps to further an audience as well.

Your honest feedback not only provides valuable insights for me but also assists fellow readers in making informed decisions about their next literary adventure. Whether it's a few sentences or a more detailed review, every contribution makes a significant impact.

Thank you for being a part of this journey with me. Your support is the driving force behind my passion for writing devotions and inspirations along with scripture from God's Word. If you have any questions or would like to share your thoughts directly with me, feel free to reach out on my website at marlenacompston.co or at my email: marlena@marlenacompston.co or on my Facebook page at InspireNations.

Wishing you joy in your reading adventures.

Marlena Compston

#thehammockseries

ABOUT THE AUTHOR

MARLENA COMPSTON is an author, speaker, and evangelist with a prophetic call. Her call and passion are for restoration to those seeking emotional and spiritual healing. She is the founder of InspireNations Media and leads a women's group, The Journey, helping women move forward from trauma and loss. Marlena is a  graduate of the University of Oklahoma and holds a degree in Organizational Leadership. To contact Marlena for speaking engagements, book signings, or more information, visit marlenacompston.co.

LOOKING AHEAD: EXPLORE *THE HAMMOCK SERIES*

Book 1: *Love Illuminated: A Devotional Journal to Awaken and Deepen Your Faith.* Immerse yourself in the heartfelt musings that spark inspiration and reflection. Join the journey of self-discovery as you unwind in the wisdom found within.

Book 2: **Coming Soon!** *Seeking His Wisdom: Inspiration and Instruction for Life.* Take the next step in our series, where inspirations are paired with practical instructions for navigating life's intricate dance. Delve deeper into the profound teachings that guide and uplift.

Book 3: **Coming Soon!** *From Glory to Glory: The Finale.* Brace yourself for the grand conclusion of our series. As we bid farewell to *The Hammock*, prepare for a captivating finale that weaves together the threads of inspiration, instruction, and the beauty of life's journey.

Stay tuned for updates and exclusive content by visiting marlenacompston. co and by following InspireNations Media on Facebook, Instagram, X, and LinkedIn. Your continued support means the world to me, and I can't wait for you to experience all three books in *The Hammock* series.

Thank you for being a part of this literary adventure!

CONNECT WITH MARLENA COMPSTON

THANK YOU for joining me on this literary journey through *Love Illuminated: A Devotional Journal to Awaken and Deepen Your Faith*.

As an author deeply passionate about the themes explored in this book, I am excited to extend my presence beyond these pages. If you are interested in bringing the insights and inspirations to life, I am available for:

Book Clubs: Invite Marlena to your book club, virtually or in-person. Explore the profound messages within the text, and share insights and reflections that enrich our collective understanding.

Speaking Engagements, Summits, and Charity Events: Invite me to share messages of faith and inspiration at your virtual or in-person events, conferences, panel discussions, and seminars.

Consulting and Coaching: I offer prophetic coaching sessions and consulting services to individuals and organizations.

For more information or to discuss potential collaborations, please reach out to marlena@marlenacompston.co or visit marlenacompston.co.

Let's continue this journey of inspiration and connection beyond the pages of the book. I look forward to the possibility of working together to awaken and deepen our faith.

Made in the USA
Monee, IL
17 June 2024

59582198R00226